CW00351209

THE OFFICIAL
CLARETS
2018/19 YEARBOOK

Contributors: Peter Rogers

A TWOCAN PUBLICATION

©2018. Published by twocan under licence from Burnley FC.

ISBN: 978-1-912692-25-5

PICTURE CREDITS: Action Images, Andy Ford, Press Association.

CONTENTS

Fixtures 2018/19	6
Burnley FC 2018/19	8
Player of the Year	10
Goal of the Year	12
Pre-Season	14
Premier League Squad 2018/19	18
Icon in Claret & Blue - Jimmy McIlroy	40
2017/18 Review	44
The Moment: Burnley are Back!	50
<<Rewind Quiz of the Year	52
10 Great Goals	54
U23 Squad 2018/19	62
Spot the Season	68
Icon in Claret & Blue - Mike Phelan	70
U18 Squad 2018/19	72
Fast Forward Predictions>>	76
Burnley Women 2018/19	78
The Moment: Danny Delivers	80
Quiz Answers	82

PREMIER LEAGUE FIXTURES

JULY 2018

Thu	26	Aberdeen	A	Europa League

AUGUST 2018

Thu	2	Aberdeen	H	Europa League
Thu	9	Istanbul Basaksehir	A	Europa League
Sun	12	Southampton	A	
Thu	16	Istanbul Basaksehir	H	Europa League
Sun	19	Watford	H	
Thu	23	Olympiakos	A	Europa League
Sun	26	Fulham	A	
Thu	30	Olympiakos	H	Europa League

SEPTEMBER 2018

Sun	2	Manchester United	H	
Sun	16	Wolverhampton Wanderers	A	
Sat	22	Bournemouth	H	
Tue	25	Burton Albion	A	Carabao Cup 3
Sun	30	Cardiff City	A	

OCTOBER 2018

Sat	6	Huddersfield Town	H	
Sat	20	Manchester City	A	
Sun	28	Chelsea	H	

NOVEMBER 2018

Sat	3	West Ham United	A	
Sat	10	Leicester City	A	
Mon	26	Newcastle United	H	

DECEMBER 2018

Sat	1	Crystal Palace	A	
Wed	5	Liverpool	H	
Sat	8	Brighton & Hove Albion	H	
Sat	15	Tottenham Hotspur	A	
Sat	22	Arsenal	A	
Wed	26	Everton	H	
Sun	30	West Ham United	H	

2018/19

JANUARY 2019

Wed	2	Huddersfield Town	A	
Sat	5			FA Cup 3
Sat	12	Fulham	H	
Sat	19	Watford	A	
Sat	26			FA Cup 4
Tue	29	Manchester United	A	

FEBRUARY 2019

Sat	2	Southampton	H	
Sat	9	Brighton & Hove Albion	A	
Sat	16			FA Cup 5
Sat	23	Tottenham Hotspur	H	
Wed	27	Newcastle United	A	

MARCH 2019

Sat	2	Crystal Palace	H	
Sat	9	Liverpool	A	
Sat	16	Leicester City	H	FA Cup 6
Sat	30	Wolverhampton Wanderers	H	

APRIL 2019

Sat	6	Bournemouth	A	FA Cup SF
Sat	13	Cardiff City	H	
Sat	20	Chelsea	A	
Sat	27	Manchester City	H	

MAY 2019

Sat	4	Everton	A	
Sun	12	Arsenal	H	
Sat	18			FA Cup Final

Fixtures are subject to change.

Back Row (L-R): Aaron Lennon, Robbie Brady, Phil Bardsley, Dwight McNeil, Nick Pope, James Tarkowski, Ben Gibson, Joe Hart, Stephen Ward, Matej Vydra, Ashley Westwood, Steven Defour.

Middle Row (L-R): Pablo Sanchez, Charlie Taylor, Jack Cork, Jeff Hendrick, Sam Vokes, Adam Legzdins, Kevin Long, Tom Heaton, Ben Mee, Anders Lindegaard, Chris Wood, Ashley Barnes, Matt Lowton, Johann Berg Gudmundsson, Dan Morrison.

Front Row (L-R): Iain Worton, Elliott Frankland, Ally Beattie, Tom Short, Billy Mercer, Tony Loughlan, Sean Dyche, Ian Woan, Mark Howard, Adam Fairclough, Phil Pomeroy, Lee Martin, Ronan Kavanagh.

BURNLEY FC
2018/19

9

Nick Pope was crowned the Clarets' Player of the Year for 2017/18.

And to cap an outstanding first season as a Premier League regular, the Clarets' goalkeeper made his England debut and won a place in the Three Lions' squad for the 2018 World Cup finals in Russia.

Pope topped a pole of thousands of votes cast by supporters via the club's official website to win the overall player of the year prize from a shortlist which included Ashley Barnes, James Tarkowski and Ben Mee.

PLAYER OF THE YEAR 17/18

His performances over the season - which saw the 26-year-old keep twelve clean sheets to help the Clarets earn a place in the Europa League and receive his first call-up to the full England squad - also earned him the recognition of his teammates who confirmed his as the Players' Player of the Year.

When reflecting on the season, the popular 'keeper admitted it had been an incredible adventure.

"It's something I could never have imagined. It's been an unbelievable year," said Pope.

"No player, fan or pundit could have imagined we'd be sitting here in seventh place with Europe guaranteed," he added when speaking the club's end-of-season awards event.

"It's a massive achievement, so to be here with these awards I'm massively proud. It's a team effort, people off the bench and the squad as well. The players and the staff - particularly goalkeeping coach Billy Mercer - have looked after me down to a man. They are the ones in front of me, putting their bodies on the line on a Saturday or helping me out. I can't thank them enough."

Pope was also swift to pay tribute to the club's fans who backed him and his teammates to the hilt throughout a memorable campaign.

"It makes a massive difference to a player when you know you've got the fans on side. From day one, they've been on my side and supported me and the team, so I can't thank them enough."

Pope's sudden rise to fame came when Tom Heaton was injured in the first-half of the Clarets' match at home to Crystal Palace on 10 September 2017. That moment signalled Pope's Premier League debut, as he entered the fray and kept a clean sheet in a 1-0 victory over the Eagles. Until then, Pope had made just four first-team appearances for Burnley following his involvement in the previous season's League Cup and FA Cup ties.

Although the thoughts of everyone at the club were with Heaton following the news that his injury was of a long-term nature, Pope immediately stepped up to the plate and grabbed his opportunity to shine on the Premier League stage. He marked his first Premier League start with an impressive display in a 1-1 draw away to Liverpool.

His shot-stopping, handling and organisational skills, swiftly instilled confidence in the Clarets' defence and won him rave reviews.

Pope's twelve Premier League clean sheets played a vital part in the Clarets securing a seventh-placed finish and qualification for the 2018/19 Europa League.

Pope's form at club level saw him named in the England squad for the first time in March 2018 and his international debut came in a 2-0 victory over Costa Rica in a World Cup warm-up match at Elland Road, before Pope proudly boarded the plane for England's memorable summer in Russia.

GOAL OF THE SEASON
17/18

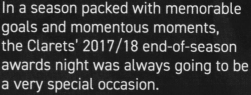

In a season packed with memorable goals and momentous moments, the Clarets' 2017/18 end-of-season awards night was always going to be a very special occasion.

The celebration evening was attended by almost 900 supporters and saw Steven Defour win the Goal of the Season award for his magnificent free-kick in the Clarets' Boxing Day draw at Manchester United.

Defour's strike led the vote taken on the evening from a magnificent top ten goals which lit up the Clarets' 2017/18 campaign.

A Boxing Day trip to Old Trafford appeared to be one of the toughest looking assignments of the season when the Clarets' fixture schedule was released back in June 2017. However, Sean Dyche's men took the 2017/18 season by storm and travelled to Old Trafford brimming with confidence on the back of some highly impressive results and performances during the opening months of the season.

Striker Ashley Barnes, who himself collected a Centurion award on the evening having made his 100th appearances for the club during the 2017/18 season, fired the Clarets ahead after only three minutes against Jose Mourinho's men. Then nine minutes before the break, Defour struck what was to become Burnley's goal of the season to make it 2-0.

Remarkably, the goal was Defour's first of the season, and to say it was worth the wait would be something of an understatement. Burnley won a free-kick in a central position, some 30 yards from goal, and up stepped the talented Belgian to send a superb effort right into the top corner.

The quality of the strike left United's Spanish international 'keeper David de Gea clutching at thin air. A truly sublime free-kick, the strike even had sections of home supporters in the Stretford End applauding. While at the other end of Old Trafford, the travelling Clarets fans knew they had witnessed something very special.

The brilliance of Defour's free-kick alone really should have been enough for Burnley to secure an Old Trafford victory. Sadly, a second-half brace from Jesse Lingard saw the points shared.

The Clarets left Old Trafford feeling a touch unfortunate not to have won the game, but regardless of two dropped points from a winning position, Defour's free-kick provided a moment of Burnley history that will live long in the memory.

In total Defour featured in 24 Premier League games last season and produced several polished performances as the Clarets sealed their remarkable seventh-place finish in the table.

The Clarets' preparations for the 2018/19 season were certainly geared towards the team's hectic schedule of fixtures during the opening weeks of the new campaign.

PRE SEASON 18/19

JIMMY DUNNE'S WINNER V CORK CITY

The summer build-up work was all carefully put in place to ensure Sean Dyche's squad would be equipped to hit the ground running as they prepared to tackle the joint challenges of Europa League football and the Premier League in 2018/19.

As the Clarets headed out to Ireland for a week-long training camp just outside Dublin, the 2018 World Cup finals in Russia were heading towards a conclusion. In fact Burnley's first game of pre-season took place just 48 hours after England's semi-final defeat to Croatia.

In front of a crowd of just over 1,700 the Clarets ended a good week away with a positive workout. Boss Dyche was able to field a different side in each half with almost all of the travelling party enjoying 45 minutes action. The match against Cork City at Turner's Cross witnessed a welcome return to action for Tom Heaton, whose shoulder injury suffered in September 2017 had ultimately cost him a World Cup place. In truth the Burnley 'keeper was never really tested against the defending League of Ireland champions.

The match was settled by a single goal which came from Clarets' young Irish defender Jimmy Dunne 20 minutes from time. The goal was Dunne's first senior strike and came following a successful loan spell with Accrington Stanley at the end of the previous season.

Upon their return to the Barnfield Training Centre, Dyche spilt his squad into two groups for simultaneous evening fixtures at Macclesfield Town and Curzon Ashton on Friday 20 July.

In front of boss Dyche at Moss Rose, goals from Aaron Lennon and Johann Berg Gudmundsson, back from his World Cup adventure with Iceland, secured a 2-0 victory over Football League new boys Macclesfield.

Meanwhile at Curzon Ashton's Tameside Stadium, Robbie Brady made his first public appearance in a Burnley shirt since a season-ending knee injury in December as the visitors ran out 5-2 winners against their National League North hosts. The goals came from Sam Vokes (2), Ben Mee, Nahki Wells and Jon Walters.

Although the Clarets were due to have two further pre-season friendly matches to play ahead of their Premier League opener at Southampton, their next assignment away to Championship side Preston North End was their final warm-up fixture prior to the commencement of the Europa League Qualifying campaign. With the club's eagerly anticipated return to European football handing them an all-British second round qualifying tie with Scottish Premier League side Aberdeen, Dons' boss Derek McInnes was an interested onlooker at Deepdale on Monday 23 July just three days before the two sides were due to meet at Pittodrie.

Aaron Lennon scored for the second game running as the Clarets completed their public preparations for their return to Europe with an entertaining 3-2 victory, secured by Dwight McNeil's late strike.

DWIGHT McNEIL CELEBRATES SCORING THE WINNER AT DEEPDALE

AARON LENNON

15

SAM VOKES NETS AT PITTODRIE

CELEBRATIONS AFTER
VOKES EQUALISES IN THE
EUROPA LEAGUE FIRST LEG
MATCH AGAINST ABERDEEN

With manager Dyche having to balance the demands of the start of Burnley's Europa League campaign with the Premier League kick-off in almost three weeks' time, he utilised 22 players at Deepdale as the Clarets came from behind to seal victory with second-half goals - and their first at senior level - from young substitutes McNeil and Dan Agyei.

North End started well and went in front after 22 minutes when Sean Maguire picked out Josh Harrop to steer a low shot into the bottom corner. The Clarets were not behind for long though and levelled a minute later when Jeff Hendrick saw a goal-bound effort blocked and Lennon pounced on the rebound to lash home.

Burnley completed the turnaround after 72 minutes, following widespread changes in personnel. Agyei had seen one headed chance saved earlier on, but gave Declan Rudd no chance with a thumping header from a Jon Walters cross.

This time, however, Burnley were the ones to relinquish the lead quickly as Preston hit back to level as Callum Robinson capitalised on hesitation in the Clarets' defence to guide a shot past substitute 'keeper Adam Legzdins.

Burnley had the final word six minutes from the end of an entertaining game when McNeil again showed his potential with a classy left-foot finish curled home on the volley to send Burnley north of the border on a winning note.

After the Europa League adventure began with a 1-1 draw at Pittodrie, the Clarets switched attentions back to their Premier League preparations with a visit from French top-flight side Montpellier being sandwiched in between the two Aberdeen fixtures.

In what was the first of three games at Turf Moor in the space of six days, a sparse crowd of 4,162 witnessed a goalless draw with Montpellier that was marred by the latest leg of Brady's comeback being cut-short. The Republic of Ireland international was withdrawn just before half-time as a precautionary measure after feeling a slight problem with his hamstring.

The second leg of the Europa League tie with Aberdeen provided a full-blooded Anglo-Scottish tussle which Burnley eventually won 3-1 after extra-time on what was a pulsating evening at Turf Moor.

Next up on Saturday 5 August was the final game of the club's pre-season programme. After all that went into conquering the 'Battle of Britain' less than 48 hours earlier, Dyche opted to rest those that had been through the 120-minute test against the Dons when Spanish outfit Espanyol visited Turf Moor. With new signing Ben Gibson watching on, the Clarets rounded off their pre-season with a low-key 2-0 Turf Moor defeat to a strong Espanyol side.

The success over Aberdeen handed the Clarets a place in the third qualifying round of the Europa League and that resulted in a trip to Turkey to face Istanbul Basaksehir ahead of the Premier League opener at St Mary's on Sunday 12 August 2018.

JACK CORK WITH THE SECOND

CHRIS WOOD TAKES THE APPLAUSE AFTER OPENING THE SCORING AT HOME TO THE DONS

PREMIER LEAGUE SQUAD 2018/19

POSITION: Goalkeeper
DoB: 15 April 1986
COUNTRY: England

Much-travelled and experienced goalkeeper Tom Heaton became Sean Dyche's first permanent signing as Burnley manager when Heaton arrived at Turf Moor in the summer of 2013.

Since joining the club, Heaton has helped the Clarets enjoy a sustained period of success. Promotion to the Premier League was secured in 2013/14 and Heaton's performances the following season at top-flight level won him the Players' Player of the Year award despite the team's return to the Championship.

Dyche named Heaton as captain for the 2015/16 season and the 'keeper played a vital role in the Clarets' immediate return to the Premier League after landing the Championship title.

His form at club level saw him win an England cap in the summer of 2016 and his consistency for the Clarets was rewarded with a new improved four-year contract, securing his services at Turf Moor until 2020.

An outstanding performer in 2016/17 as the Clarets retained their Premier League status, Heaton suffered a shoulder injury against Crystal Palace in September 2017 that ruled him out for the remainder of the 2017/18 season.

He returned to the Burnley team for the Europa League matches with Olympiakos in August 2018.

1
TOM HEATON

2
MATTHEW LOWTON

POSITION: Defender

DoB: 9 June 1989

COUNTRY: England

Defender Matthew Lowton joined the Clarets in the summer of 2015 and played a vital role in helping Burnley secure promotion back to the Premier League at the first time of asking in 2015/16.

Having began his career with Sheffield United, Lowton gained Premier League experience during a three-year spell with Aston Villa. He was a star performer at Villa Park under the management of Paul Lambert and after impressing during his first season in the second city, he was handed an improved and extended contract.

With the ability to operate in a right-back berth or in central defence, Lowton's flexibility and previous top-flight experience has seen him become one of the first names on manager Sean Dyche's teamsheet and a highly-respected member of the Clarets' squad.

As the 2018/19 campaign got underway, Lowton was closing in on his 100th appearance in a Burnley shirt and the popular 29-year-old looks all set to collect a centurion award at club's end-of-season awards.

19

3
CHARLIE TAYLOR

POSITION: Defender
DoB: 18 September 1993
COUNTRY: England

Left-back Charlie Taylor joined Burnley in July 2017 after agreeing a four-year deal at Turf Moor following the end of his contract at Leeds United.

York-born Taylor began his career at Elland Road and progressed through the Leeds United Academy to the first team. During his time at Leeds, Taylor took in valuable loan spells with Bradford City, York City, Inverness Caledonian Thistle and Fleetwood Town before cementing himself a place in the first team at Elland Road.

After over a century of first-team appearances for Leeds, Taylor jumped at the opportunity of plying his trade in the Premier League when the Clarets came calling in the summer of 2017.

He made his Burnley debut in the white-hot atmosphere of an East Lancashire derby away to Blackburn in the League Cup. After tasting the joy of victory over the arch-enemy, Taylor went on to feature in eleven Premier League fixtures as Burnley defied the odds to secure seventh place and bring European football back to Turf Moor.

4
JACK CORK

POSITION: Midfielder
DoB: 25 June 1989
COUNTRY: England

A key performer in the Clarets' 2017/18 success, midfielder Jack Cork played in every minute of every Premier League game as Burnley recorded their best league finish since 1974.

Cork rejoined Burnley for a second spell at the club in July 2017 after agreeing a switch from Premier League rivals Swansea City. He had previously made 57 appearances for the Clarets while on loan from Chelsea between January 2010 and May 2011.

A former England U21 international, Cork, the son former Wimbledon striker Alan, began his career at Chelsea. During his time at Stamford Bridge, Cork was loaned to AFC Bournemouth, Scunthorpe United, Southampton, Watford and Coventry City as well as the Clarets.

He finally cut his ties with Chelsea when he joined Southampton in 2011. Cork moved on to Swansea in the January 2015 transfer window and became captain at the Liberty Stadium prior to his return to Turf Moor.

His impressive performances for the Clarets were rewarded with an England call-up and he made his international debut for the Three Lions during the Wembley friendly with Germany in November 2017.

21

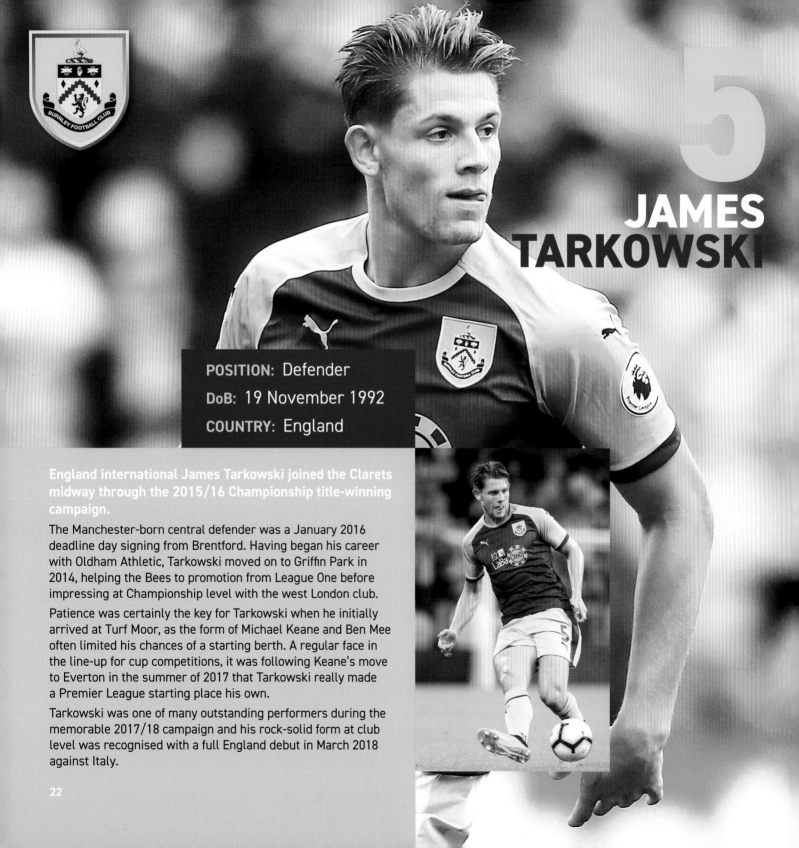

5

JAMES
TARKOWSKI

POSITION: Defender

DoB: 19 November 1992

COUNTRY: England

England international James Tarkowski joined the Clarets midway through the 2015/16 Championship title-winning campaign.

The Manchester-born central defender was a January 2016 deadline day signing from Brentford. Having began his career with Oldham Athletic, Tarkowski moved on to Griffin Park in 2014, helping the Bees to promotion from League One before impressing at Championship level with the west London club.

Patience was certainly the key for Tarkowski when he initially arrived at Turf Moor, as the form of Michael Keane and Ben Mee often limited his chances of a starting berth. A regular face in the line-up for cup competitions, it was following Keane's move to Everton in the summer of 2017 that Tarkowski really made a Premier League starting place his own.

Tarkowski was one of many outstanding performers during the memorable 2017/18 campaign and his rock-solid form at club level was recognised with a full England debut in March 2018 against Italy.

6

BEN MEE

POSITION: Defender
DoB: 21 September 1989
COUNTRY: England

An FA Youth Cup winner with Manchester City in 2008, central defender Ben Mee progressed through the Academy set-up at City before going on to play first-team football under the management of Roberto Mancini.

With regular first-team opportunities hard to come by among a squad of seasoned internationals, Mee took in a loan spell with Leicester City in January 2011.

He then joined the Clarets on a season-long loan at the beginning of the 2011/12 campaign. Such was the impression he made at Turf Moor, the deal became permanent in January 2012 when the Sale-born defender agreed a three-and-a-half year deal with Burnley.

Mee has been a consistent and reliable performer for the club from the moment he first walked through the door at Turf Moor. He has now played over 250 games in Claret and Blue. With the ability to operate at left-back as well as his preferred position in the heart of the defence, Mee remains a vital member of Sean Dyche's squad.

7
JOHANN BERG GUDMUNDSSON

POSITION: Midfielder
DoB: 27 October 1990
COUNTRY: Iceland

Burnley secured the services of attacking midfielder Johann Berg Gudmundsson from Charlton Athletic in the summer of 2016 ahead of the club's return to Premier League football following their Championship title success in 2015/16.

Gudmundsson agreed a three-year deal at Turf Moor after a number of impressive performances in Iceland's remarkable surge to the quarter-finals of Euro 2016.

An attacking midfielder, Gudmundsson has won over 50 caps for Iceland and back in 2013, he became the first Icelandic player in over 13 years to net a hat-trick for his country - his treble coming in a thrilling 4-4 draw with Switzerland during World Cup qualifying.

His first season at Turf Moor was interrupted by injury, but he still managed 20 Premier League appearances as Burnley maintained their top-flight status.

Last season saw him start 32 league games and net a memorable goal in the 1-1 draw at home to champions-elect Manchester City, before going on to represent his country at the 2018 World Cup finals in Russia.

9
SAM VOKES

POSITION: Striker

DoB: 21 October 1989

COUNTRY: Wales

With over 250 appearances and more than half a century of goals for the Clarets, Welsh international striker Sam Vokes has gained legendary status at Turf Moor.

Vokes joined the club on a permanent basis in the summer of 2012 having spent a two-month spell with the Clarets during the 2011/12 season, when he netted twice in nine games while on loan from Wolverhampton Wanderers.

A powerful target-man with great awareness of those around him, Vokes was very much the focal point of the Clarets' attack during their promotion seasons of 2013/14 and 2015/16.

He has carried his good form into the Premier League and his opening day brace at Chelsea last season did so much to set the tone for the season ahead. Not always a starter, due to the form of fellow strikers Ashley Barnes and Chris Wood, Vokes scored four Premier League goals in 2017/18, including the winner away to boyhood club Southampton.

10
ASHLEY BARNES

POSITION: Striker

DoB: 30 October 1989

COUNTRY: Austria

Striker Ashley Barnes joined the Clarets in January 2014 and helped his new club clinch promotion to the Premier League just five months after his arrival.

After joining from Brighton & Hove Albion and agreeing a three-and-a-half-year deal, Barnes scored the first goal in the 2-0 victory over Wigan at Turf Moor that secured promotion.

After scoring five goals at Premier League level in 2014/15, he suffered a serious knee injury that ruled him out for the majority of the 2015/16 Championship campaign. With the Clarets back in the Premier League, Barnes netted his first goal in 20 months to seal a late win at Crystal Palace in November 2016 - that was one of six league goals he scored as Sean Dyche's men maintained their Premier League status with a 16th-place finish come the end of the 2016/17 campaign.

Last season was a major success for Barnes as he hit double figures, with nine in the Premier League, as the club secured its best league finish in 44 years.

11
CHRIS WOOD

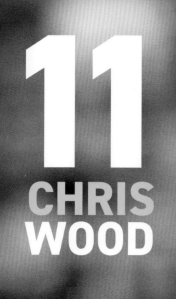

POSITION: Striker
DoB: 7 December 1991
COUNTRY: New Zealand

New Zealand striker Chris Wood moved into English football when he joined West Bromwich Albion in 2009. However, he took on a rather nomadic existence while on the books at the Hawthorns as he was on loan to six different clubs before securing a permanent move to Leicester City.

While with the Foxes netted 20 goals from 62 appearances and was also loaned to Ipswich Town before joining Leeds United in July 2015. He was prolific in front of goal across two seasons at Elland Road, bagging an impressive 41 goals from 83 Championship outings, form that earned him a big money move to the Premier League and the Clarets in August 2017.

His arrival at Turf Moor set a new record transfer for Burnley and Wood soon began to repay the club's investment - marking his debut with a Wembley equaliser to secure a Premier League point away to Tottenham Hotspur.

He ended his maiden season at Turf Moor as leading scorer with eleven goals despite missing a chunk of the campaign with injury.

27

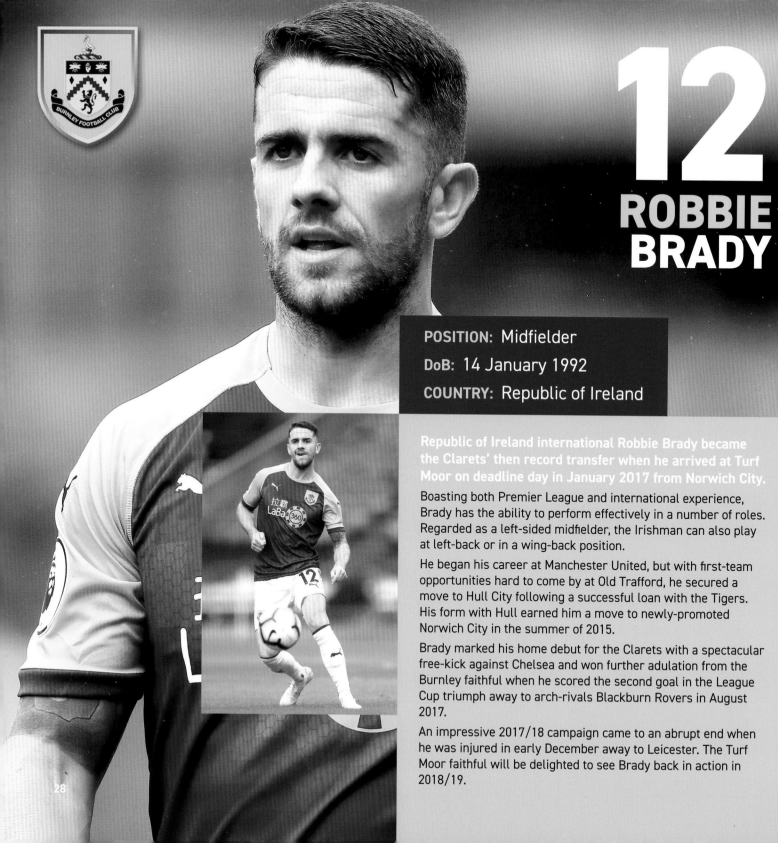

12
ROBBIE BRADY

POSITION: Midfielder
DoB: 14 January 1992
COUNTRY: Republic of Ireland

Republic of Ireland international Robbie Brady became the Clarets' then record transfer when he arrived at Turf Moor on deadline day in January 2017 from Norwich City.

Boasting both Premier League and international experience, Brady has the ability to perform effectively in a number of roles. Regarded as a left-sided midfielder, the Irishman can also play at left-back or in a wing-back position.

He began his career at Manchester United, but with first-team opportunities hard to come by at Old Trafford, he secured a move to Hull City following a successful loan with the Tigers. His form with Hull earned him a move to newly-promoted Norwich City in the summer of 2015.

Brady marked his home debut for the Clarets with a spectacular free-kick against Chelsea and won further adulation from the Burnley faithful when he scored the second goal in the League Cup triumph away to arch-rivals Blackburn Rovers in August 2017.

An impressive 2017/18 campaign came to an abrupt end when he was injured in early December away to Leicester. The Turf Moor faithful will be delighted to see Brady back in action in 2018/19.

13

JEFF HENDRICK

POSITION: Midfielder

DoB: 31 January 1992

COUNTRY: Republic of Ireland

Burnley Football Club will certainly always have a special place in the heart of Jeff Hendrick - it was against the Clarets that Hendrick made his Football League debut for Derby County back in April 2011.

The goalscoring midfielder joined the Rams' Academy and progressed through their youth and reserve teams before turning professional at Pride Park in 2010. During his time in the East Midlands, Hendrick netted 27 goals from midfield to become a real crowd favourite.

The Republic of Ireland international joined the Clarets in the summer of 2016 following the club's promotion to the Premier League. After securing a then record-breaking move to Turf Moor, Hendrick swiftly became a regular starter for Sean Dyche's side and he landed the Clarets' Goal of the Season award for his spectacular volley in the 3-2 victory over Bournemouth at Turf Moor.

His excellent form continued as he featured in all but four matches in Burnley's memorable 2017/18 Premier League campaign.

29

14
BEN
GIBSON

POSITION: Defender
DoB: 15 January 1993
COUNTRY: England

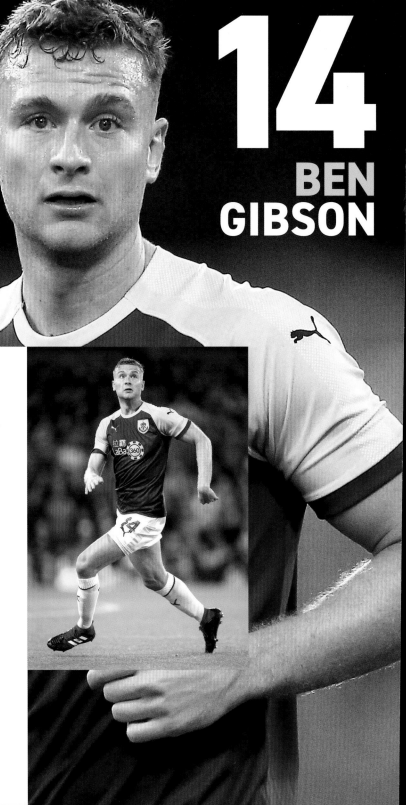

Burnley completed the signing of England U21 defender Ben Gibson from Middlesbrough for a joint club record fee in August 2018.

He arrived at Turf Moor with Premier League experience under his belt having featured in Boro's 2016/17 campaign. Widely regarded as one of the best defenders outside of the top-flight, securing his services was seen as a major coup for Burnley.

Teesside-born Gibson, nephew of Boro chairman Steve, progressed through Boro's successful youth system before going on to make over 200 first-team appearances for the Riverside club.

Gibson was a key member of the Boro side that suffered a 2-0 Play-Off Final defeat to Norwich City in 2014/15, before playing his part in promotion the following season as Boro landed the runners-up spot behind Burnley.

With Boro suffering an immediate return to the Championship, Gibson stayed loyal to his hometown club as they reached the Play-Offs again in 2017/18, but after falling at the semi-final stage, he was delighted to be able to return to the Premier League with Burnley.

His Clarets' debut came at Turf Moor as Burnley edged past Istanbul Buyuk in the Europa League.

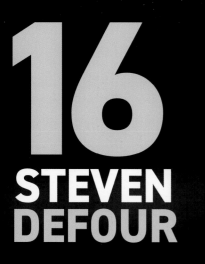

16
STEVEN DEFOUR

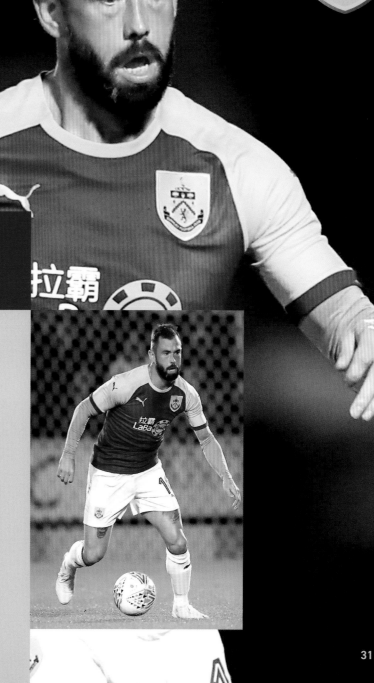

POSITION: Midfielder
DoB: 15 April 1988
COUNTRY: Belgium

A firm fans' favourite at Turf Moor, Belgian international midfielder Steven Defour joined Burnley in the summer of 2016 for a then club-record fee from Anderlecht.

Defour is a player who is certainly capable of producing moments of magic that get supporters up off their seats and he netted the Clarets' 2017/18 Goal of the Season with a stunning free-kick in the thrilling 2-2 draw with Manchester United at Old Trafford on Boxing Day 2017.

Born in Mechelen, 30-year-old Defour began his professional career with Genk before moving on to Standard Liege, Porto and Anderlecht.

He agreed a three-year deal with the Clarets in August 2016 after finally making his long sought-after move to the Premier League. He marked his maiden campaign at Turf Moor with memorable goals against Hull City and Bristol City (FA Cup) as the Clarets maintained their top-flight status.

The 2017/18 season saw the talented playmaker ever-present up until January when a knee injury required season-ending surgery.

31

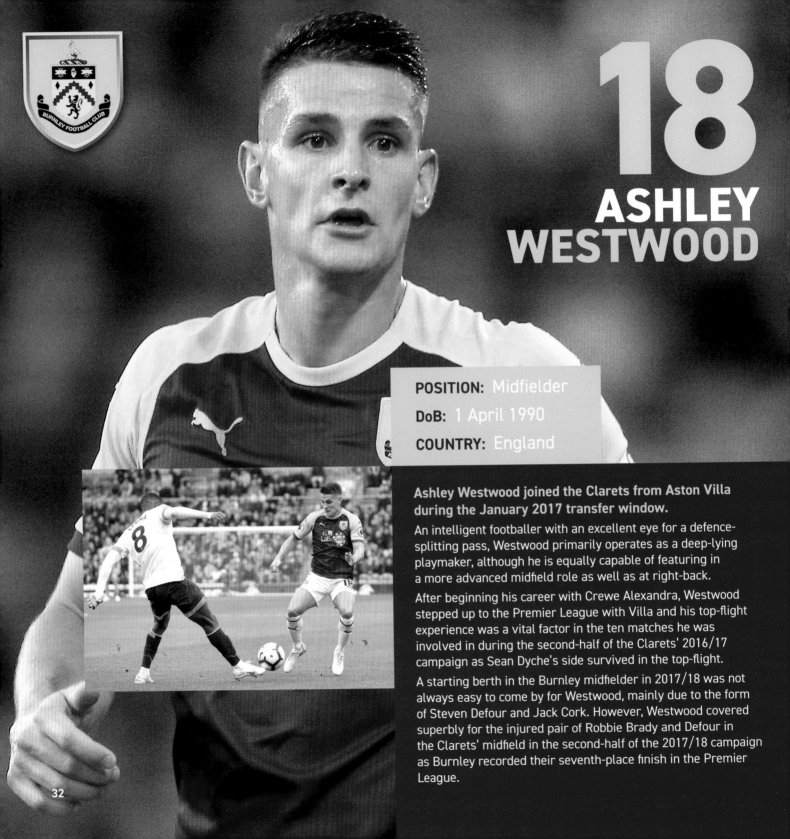

18
ASHLEY WESTWOOD

POSITION: Midfielder

DoB: 1 April 1990

COUNTRY: England

Ashley Westwood joined the Clarets from Aston Villa during the January 2017 transfer window.

An intelligent footballer with an excellent eye for a defence-splitting pass, Westwood primarily operates as a deep-lying playmaker, although he is equally capable of featuring in a more advanced midfield role as well as at right-back.

After beginning his career with Crewe Alexandra, Westwood stepped up to the Premier League with Villa and his top-flight experience was a vital factor in the ten matches he was involved in during the second-half of the Clarets' 2016/17 campaign as Sean Dyche's side survived in the top-flight.

A starting berth in the Burnley midfielder in 2017/18 was not always easy to come by for Westwood, mainly due to the form of Steven Defour and Jack Cork. However, Westwood covered superbly for the injured pair of Robbie Brady and Defour in the Clarets' midfield in the second-half of the 2017/18 campaign as Burnley recorded their seventh-place finish in the Premier League.

20
JOE
HART

POSITION: Goalkeeper
DoB: 19 April 1987
COUNTRY: England

Following Nick Pope's injury sustained in the Europa League opener at Aberdeen, boss Sean Dyche acted swiftly to enhance the goalkeeping options at Turf Moor when he swooped for vastly experienced goalkeeper Joe Hart in August 2018.

A former Premier League winner with Manchester City, Hart is a great shot-stopper whose presence certainly adds confidence to those who play in front of him. He joined the Clarets after agreeing a two-year deal, thus ending a trophy-laden twelve-year stay at the Etihad Stadium.

Hart had amassed 75 England caps when he arrived at Burnley, having made his Three Lions debut back in 2008. In pursuit of regular first-team football, he has also taken in loan spells at Torino and West Ham United before taking up the Turf Moor challenge.

First choice between the sticks as the 2018/19 Premier League season kicked off - Hart's excellent performances in the Burnley goal were a highlight of a testing start to the new campaign.

33

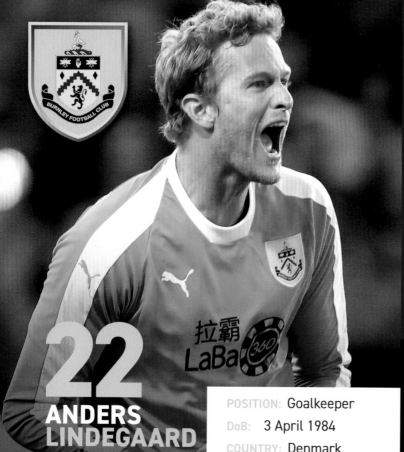

22
ANDERS LINDEGAARD

POSITION:	Goalkeeper
DoB:	3 April 1984
COUNTRY:	Denmark

Danish international goalkeeper Lindegaard provides quality competition for the number one slot at Turf Moor after the experienced 'keeper joined the Clarets in September 2017.

The big Dane was a Premier League winner with Manchester United during Sir Alex Ferguson's final season in charge at Old Trafford. He arrived at Burnley as manager Sean Dyche looked to strengthen the goalkeeping department following the injury-enforced absence of captain Tom Heaton.

Signed as a free-agent after spending the 2016/17 campaign with Preston North End, Lindegaard spent a season with West Bromwich Albion in between his time at Old Trafford and Deepdale. The 34-year-old began his career in his homeland with Odense Boldklub and played for Kolding and Aalesund before moving to England with United.

Lindergaard's Clarets' debut came when he replaced Nick Pope in the Europa League match at Aberdeen and his second outing came in the return leg at Turf Moor as Burnley progressed to the next round with a 4-2 aggregate success.

A versatile and experienced defender, Stephen Ward is one of the club's longest-serving players having joined the Clarets in August 2014 ahead of the 2014/15 Premier League season.

Ward is another member of the club's considerable Irish contingent, with the Dublin-born defender beginning his career with League of Ireland side Bohemians before earning a move to Wolverhampton Wanderers in 2007.

After playing almost 250 games for Wolves and spending a season on loan at Brighton & Hove Albion, Ward then made the move to Turf Moor. A key performer as the Clarets secured a swift return to the Premier League in 2015/16, Ward missed only one Premier League game in 2016/17.

A memorable goal gave the Clarets a two-goal lead as Burnley beat Champions Chelsea 3-2 on the opening day of the 2017/18 season. A result and performance that triggered a memorable campaign.

Ward made 28 Premier League appearances in the club's surge to a seventh-place finish and he looks set to form an important part of the Burnley backline again in 2018/19.

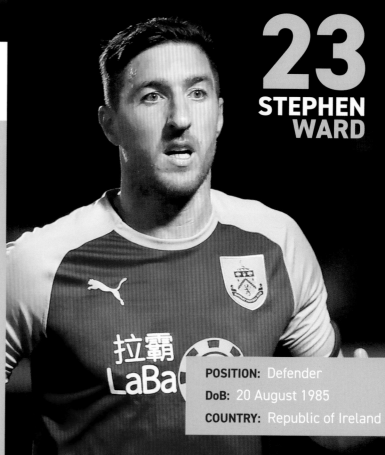

23
STEPHEN WARD

POSITION:	Defender
DoB:	20 August 1985
COUNTRY:	Republic of Ireland

25
AARON LENNON

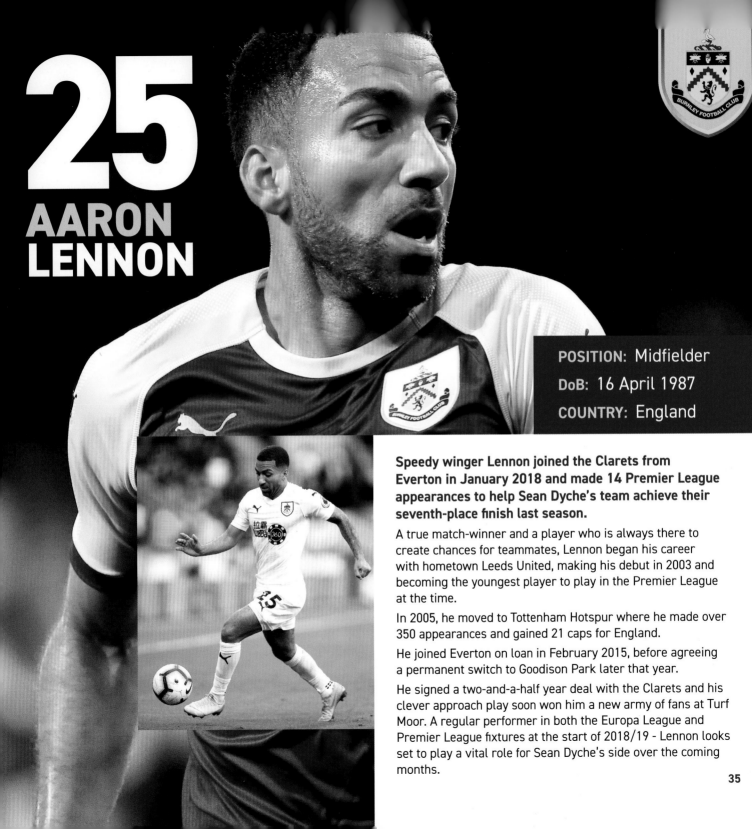

POSITION: Midfielder
DoB: 16 April 1987
COUNTRY: England

Speedy winger Lennon joined the Clarets from Everton in January 2018 and made 14 Premier League appearances to help Sean Dyche's team achieve their seventh-place finish last season.

A true match-winner and a player who is always there to create chances for teammates, Lennon began his career with hometown Leeds United, making his debut in 2003 and becoming the youngest player to play in the Premier League at the time.

In 2005, he moved to Tottenham Hotspur where he made over 350 appearances and gained 21 caps for England.

He joined Everton on loan in February 2015, before agreeing a permanent switch to Goodison Park later that year.

He signed a two-and-a-half year deal with the Clarets and his clever approach play soon won him a new army of fans at Turf Moor. A regular performer in both the Europa League and Premier League fixtures at the start of 2018/19 - Lennon looks set to play a vital role for Sean Dyche's side over the coming months.

2 P
BARDS

POSITION: Defender
DoB: 28 June 1985
COUNTRY: Scotland

Just like Turf Moor teammate Jack Cork, defender Phil Bardsley is also enjoying a second spell with the Clarets.

Bardsley initially played for the club while on loan from Manchester United during the 2005/06 season when he made six Championship appearances for the club. The 2005/06 campaign also saw Bardsley make his Premier League debut for United. After progressing through the youth ranks at Old Trafford, Bardsley made a total of 18 first-team appearances for the Red Devils and also gained first-team experience following loans at Royal Antwerp, Glasgow Rangers, Aston Villa and Sheffield United as well as here at Turf Moor.

In a bid to secure regular first-team football and a settled location, he joined Sunderland in 2008 and made 200 appearances for the Black Cats. He moved to Stoke City in 2014 before the reliable defender and Scottish international returned to Turf Moor for his second spell with the Clarets in July 2017.

27
MATEJ
VYDRA

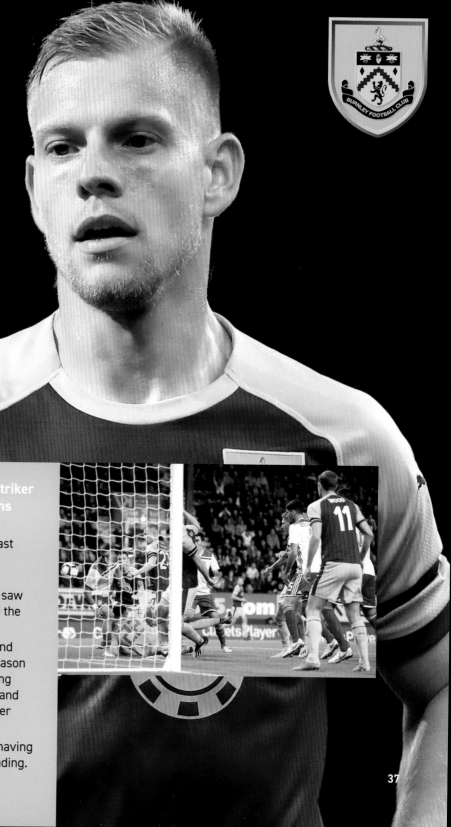

POSITION: Striker

DoB: 1 May 1992

COUNTRY: Czech Republic

Burnley swooped for Czech Republic international striker Vydra in August 2018 to boost their attacking options ahead of the 2018/19 campaign.

He scored 22 goals in all competitions for Derby County last season and marked his Burnley debut with a goal against Olympiakos in the Europa League.

Vydra's impressive 22-goal haul for the Rams in 2017/18 saw him voted Derby's Player of the Season. He also collected the Championship's Golden Boot as the division's top scorer.

His goalscoring form certainly won him many admirers, and after the Rams missed out on promotion via the end-of-season Play-Offs, Vydra swiftly became a wanted man. His finishing qualities were there for all to see throughout last season and it came of little surprise when he stepped up to the Premier League after making a summer switch to Burnley.

Vydra boasts a wealth of experience in the English game having also represented Watford, West Bromwich Albion and Reading.

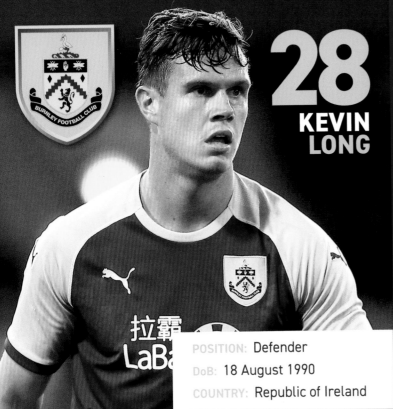

28
KEVIN LONG

POSITION:	Defender
DoB:	18 August 1990
COUNTRY:	Republic of Ireland

Recruited from Cork City back in January 2010, Kevin Long is currently the longest-serving player at Turf Moor.

A new three-year deal signed in August 2017 should result in a decade of service to the Clarets and a thoroughly well-deserved testimonial season.

Long began his career with League of Ireland side Cork and the Clarets fought off interest from a number of interested clubs to land the defender's signature during the 2010 January transfer window.

After spending his initial months at Burnley in the reserve team, Long then took in loan spells with local neighbours Accrington Stanley and also Rochdale. The 2012/13 season began with Long on loan at Portsmouth before he returned to Turf Moor and made his first senior start in December 2012.

During a lengthy Clarets career, Long has played his part in two promotion-winning campaigns and also taken in additional loan spells at Barnsley and MK Dons.

His form at the heart of the Burnley defence has been rewarded with eight full caps at international level for the Republic of Ireland.

After a total of 23 outings for club and country last season, Ward was certainly a proud participant in the club's 2018/19 Europa League campaign.

After injury ruled Tom Heaton out of action from September onwards last season, Nick Pope stepped up and produced a string of impressive displays in the Burnley goal as the Clarets secured a remarkable seventh-placed finish.

His club form saw him voted Player of the Season at Turf Moor and earned him a place in England's World Cup squad for Russia 2018.

Pope arrived at Burnley in July 2016 from Charlton Athletic, on the same day as his former Addicks' teammate Johann Berg Gudmundsson. The Soham-born stopper, who began his career with Ipswich Town, signed a three-year deal at Turf Moor.

During his time at The Valley, he was loaned to a host of clubs including Harrow Borough, Welling United, Cambridge United, Aldershot Town, York City and Bury before enjoying a prolonged spell in the Charlton first-team.

Pope's first season at Turf Moor saw him primarily used as cup 'keeper and he kept clean sheets in the FA Cup ties with Sunderland and Bristol City.

Heaton's misfortune handed Pope his chance last season and the 26-year-old certainly made the most of the opportunity that came his way.

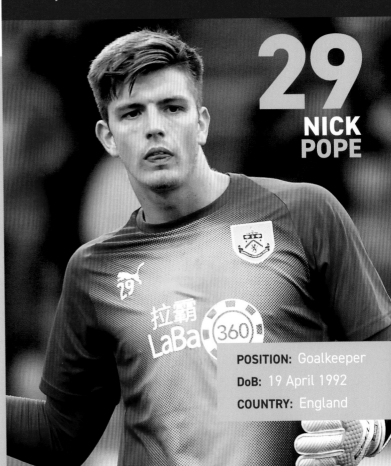

29
NICK POPE

POSITION:	Goalkeeper
DoB:	19 April 1992
COUNTRY:	England

Much-travelled goalkeeper Adam Legzdins joined the Clarets from Birmingham City ahead of the 2017/18 campaign.

With assured handling skills and excellent reflexes, Legzdins adds depth to the Clarets' goalkeeping options and will be keen to push for first-team involvement in 2018/19.

Legzdins began his career with Birmingham City and turned professional with Blues, but failed to make the breakthrough to the first-team during his first spell at St Andrew's.

After a number of loan moves, the goalkeeper joined Crewe Alexandra on a permanent basis in the summer of 2009. He has subsequently kept goal for Burton Albion, Derby County and Leyton Orient before he returned to Birmingham City in June 2017. In his second spell at Birmingham, he finally tasted first-team football for Blues, making 21 appearances in all competitions prior to his switch to Burnley.

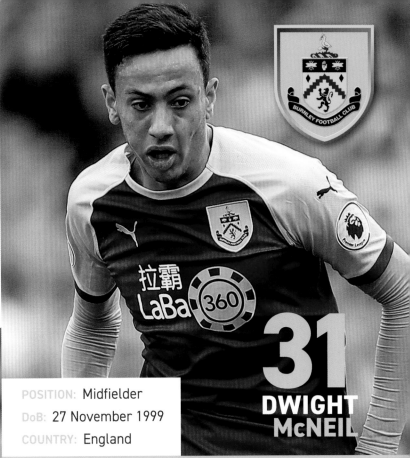

POSITION: Midfielder
DoB: 27 November 1999
COUNTRY: England

31 DWIGHT McNEIL

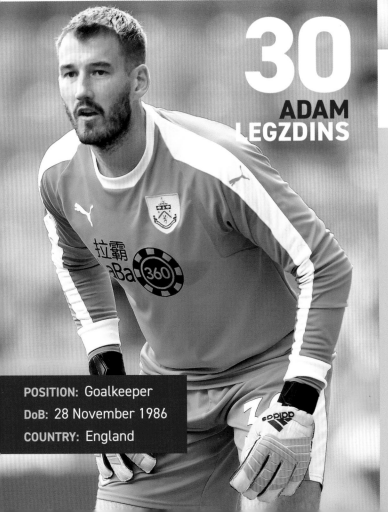

30 ADAM LEGZDINS

POSITION: Goalkeeper
DoB: 28 November 1986
COUNTRY: England

Attacking midfielder Dwight McNeil progressed through the Clarets' Academy and made his first-team debut with a late substitute appearance on the final day of the 2017/18 campaign as Bournemouth provided the opposition at Turf Moor.

McNeil joined the Academy back in 2014 after leaving Manchester United and began his two-year scholarship in the summer of 2016.

Last season, he was a leading performer for the U23 development squad prior to making his first-team breakthrough. He ended last season by being voted the Clarets' Young Player of the Year and capped off a memorable campaign by putting pen to paper on his first professional contract.

McNeil has continued to make rapid progress in 2018/19 after being handed starts in both the Europa League and the Premier League by manager Sean Dyche.

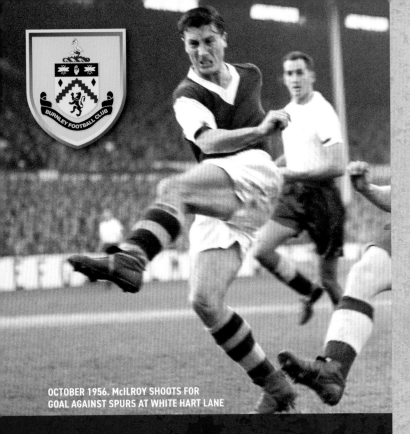

OCTOBER 1956. McILROY SHOOTS FOR GOAL AGAINST SPURS AT WHITE HART LANE

ICON
IN CLARET AND BLUE

The calendar year of 2018 will certainly be reflected upon with mixed emotions by the Turf Moor faithful.

On the pitch, manager Sean Dyche and his players secured a remarkable seventh-place finish in the Premier League - an achievement that saw the club secure its highest league placing since 1974 and the return of competitive European Football to Turf Moor for the first time in 51 years.

However, among all the excitement and pride that has been generated from the club's success in 2018, the year also saw Burnley suffer a great loss following the death of club legend Jimmy McIlroy.

McIlroy played 497 games for the Clarets between 1950 and 1962, winning the old First Division title in 1960. He was widely acknowledged as Burnley Football Club's 'greatest ever player'.

He died aged 86 on Monday 20th August, 2018. The Northern Irishman spent 13 years at Turf Moor in what was a golden era for the club. He was an integral part of Burnley's 1960 Championship-winning team under legendary manager Harry Potts.

An inside-forward who wore the number eight and number ten shirt in a period of outstanding service to the club, McIlroy scored 131 goals as the Clarets became one of the best teams in the country.

After signing from Glentoran in March 1950, McIlroy, made his Burnley debut under the management of Frank Hill in October 1950 in a First Division game at Sunderland.

A wonderfully skilful and creative player, McIlroy went on to become a mainstay of the side that did not finish outside the top seven in the First Division between 1956 and 1963 - the year he left the club to join Stoke City in a move that devastated the club's supporters.

Potts took over as manager in 1958 and with the inspirational McIlroy heading a team of talents, including club legends Adam Blacklaw, John Angus, Alex Elder, Tommy Cummings, Brian Miller, Jimmy Adamson, John Connelly, Ray Pointer, Jimmy Robson and Brian Pilkington, Burnley were crowned league champions for only the second time in their history in 1960.

40

JIMMY McILROY

1931-2018

JIMMY McILROY

1931-2018

That earned Burnley a place in Europe, McIlroy starring as the Clarets reached the quarter-finals of the European Cup the following season.

And in 1962, McIlroy and his teammates almost became only the second team to win 'The Double' - finishing second in the league to Ipswich Town and losing in the final of the FA Cup to holders and great rivals Tottenham Hotspur, who retained the trophy after winning the League and Cup twelve months earlier.

McIlroy was also one of Northern Ireland's finest players, winning 55 caps and helping his country reach the quarter-finals of the 1958 World Cup in Sweden.

After ending his playing career with Oldham Athletic, McIlroy briefly managed the Latics and Bolton Wanderers. But his home remained Burnley, where he lived for the rest of his life.

McIlroy, who has a stand named after him at Turf Moor, was given the freedom of the Borough of Burnley in 2008 and made an MBE in the New Year's Honours of 2011 for his services to football and charity.

He was inducted into the Northern Ireland Football Writers' Association Hall of Fame in 2012 and the Hall of Fame at England's National Football Museum in 2014.

With the passing of Jimmy McIlroy, the Clarets lost a true club great and a part of their history. His funeral took place on Friday, 31 August 2018, when thousands of fans, many wearing Burnley shirts and scarves, lined Harry Potts Way and broke into respectful applause as the funeral procession approached Turf Moor.

NOVEMBER 1959. THE NORTHERN IRELAND FORWARD LINE OF BILLY BINGHAM, JOHN CROSSAN, WILBUR CUSH, JIMMY McILROY & PETER McPARLAND

FULL NAME:	James McIlroy
DATE OF BIRTH:	25 October 1931
PLACE OF BIRTH:	Lambeg, Northern Ireland
POSITION:	Attacking Midfielder

BURNLEY APPEARANCES	BURNLEY GOALS
497	**131**
LEAGUE: 439	LEAGUE: 116
FA CUP: 50	FA CUP: 13
LEAGUE CUP: 3	LEAGUE CUP: 1
OTHER: 5	OTHER: 1

DEBUT: **Sunderland 1 Burnley 1**
21 October 1950 · Division One

NORTHERN IRELAND

APPEARANCES	GOALS
55	**10**

DEBUT: **Northern Ireland 0 Scotland 3**
6 October 1951

REVIEW
17/18

STEPHEN WARD SMASHES HOME THE SECOND GOAL AT STAMFORD BRIDGE

The Clarets' 2017/18 season is sure to go down in Burnley folklore after Sean Dyche's men secured a remarkable seventh-place finish in the Premier League and ensured that European football would return to Turf Moor for the first time in 51 years.

After ending the 2016/17 campaign with a 40-point haul that guaranteed top-flight survival with a 16th-place finish, most outside of Turf Moor predicted that the Clarets would again be battling it out towards the bottom end of the table.

This most remarkable of seasons began with an unenviable looking opening day trip to face reigning Premier League champions Chelsea at Stamford Bridge. Against all odds, Dyche's men pulled off the 'result of the day' after a Sam Vokes brace and a Stephen Ward wonder-strike put them 3-0 up at the break.

The Champions roared back after the interval, but Burnley hung on for a 3-2 victory and landed an unexpected win after producing an attacking display that really set the standard for the season ahead.

The Turf Moor campaign began with a narrow 1-0 defeat at home to West Bromwich Albion, but the Burnley faithful swiftly forgave their heroes for their false start on home soil as they knocked arch-rivals Blackburn Rovers out of the League Cup. Dyche's men took the local bragging rights and a place in the third round draw after goals from Jack Cork and Robbie Brady secured a 2-0 win at Ewood Park.

The opening month of the season ended on a positive note as the Clarets travelled to Wembley for the first time since the 2009 Play-Off Final to face Tottenham Hotspur in the Premier League. A late Chris Wood goal ensured a share of the spoils as the encouraging start to the 2017/18 campaign continued.

Returning to action after the first international break of the season saw the Clarets secure a vital first home win of the season. However, the 1-0 victory over Crystal Palace came at a cost - an injury sustained by 'keeper and captain Tom Heaton subsequently ruled the in-form England stopper out for the remainder of the season.

Heaton's injury opened the door for Nick Pope to show his qualities at Premier League level and the Clarets' second choice 'keeper certainly made the most of his opportunity. Pope produced a heroic display as Burnley earned a valuable point with a 1-1 draw at Anfield.

September saw the League Cup campaign end following a penalty shootout against Leeds United, before the month concluded with a hard-fought goalless draw against Premier League new boys Huddersfield Town at Turf Moor.

ROBBIE BRADY CELEBRATES THE SECOND GOAL AT BLACKBURN

POPE BRILLIANT AT ANFIELD

45

JEFF HENDRICK ON TARGET AGAINST THE MAGPIES

ROBBIE BRADY CELEBRATES SCORING THE WINNER AT BOURNEMOUTH

A gallant performance from a tricky trip to Everton saw the Clarets take all three points from their visit to Goodison Park thanks to a first-half strike from Jeff Hendrick. Triumph over the Toffees was followed by a 1-1 draw at home to West Ham United and a 3-0 defeat away to impressive league leaders Manchester City.

The Clarets wrapped up another solid month with a home win over Newcastle United - Hendrick again being the goalscoring hero.

Burnley's well-drilled defence and the outstanding form of goalkeeper Pope were winning Dyche's men many plaudits. November unsurprisingly, began in the same vein as October ended with Burnley winning matches and keeping clean sheets. Sam Vokes scored the only goal of the game against his boyhood heroes to seal all three points from a 1-0 win at Southampton before Swansea were brushed aside 2-0 at Turf Moor.

The Clarets lost 1-0 to a last-gasp penalty at home to Arsenal, but Dyche's men showed their character and spirit to bounce back from that disappointment at the first available opportunity. Just three days after the Gunners smash and grab job at Turf Moor, Burnley made the long trip to Bournemouth and retuned with all three points following a highly impressive 2-1 victory on the South Coast.

A busy December began with a narrow 1-0 defeat at Leicester, before Pope and his teammates registered a hat-trick of shutouts as Watford and Stoke were beaten 1-0 respectively at Turf Moor and another point was added to the board with a goalless draw at Brighton.

A scintillating performance from England captain Harry Kane sentenced the Clarets to their heaviest defeat home defeat of the season. Kane left with the matchball after his treble inspired Spurs to a 3-0 win.

Once again there was no keeping this Burnley team down for long, Boxing Day saw them head to Old Trafford and produce another highly-impressive away display. After Ashley Barnes had stunned the Old Trafford crowd with the opener after only three minutes, Steven Defour struck what became the club's Goal of the Season to put the Clarets 2-0 up before United produced a late comeback to salvage a point.

The calendar year of 2017 ended with a second goalless draw of the season against Huddersfield, this time in Yorkshire.

The New Year began with the Clarets suffering three straight Premier League defeats and an FA Cup exit away to Manchester City. The three league reversals were all by a single goal and came at home to Liverpool and Manchester United, while the away loss occurred at Crystal Palace. Once again Dyche's men dug deep to ensure the month did not become a total washout as they forced a late equalizer to ensure a point from their midweek trip to Newcastle on January 31.

ASHLEY BARNES' EARLY STRIKE AGAINST THE RED DEVILS

47

CHRIS WOOD SCORES THE SECOND V EVERTON

A JUBILANT ASHLEY BARNES AT LONDON STADIUM

48

Although January had certainly been a frustrating month, February soon saw Burnley back on track and showing signs of their pre-Christmas form. A point was gained from a Turf Moor meeting with champions-elect Manchester City. A 1-0 defeat at Swansea was then followed by a 1-1 draw at home to Southampton, when Dyche's men produced a performance that deserved so much more than a point, but their display did set the tone for the magic month of March.

Now widely regarded as the division's surprise package and pushing hard for a top-seven finish, Burnley won all three of their Premier League fixtures in March.

The month began with a 2-1 win over Everton at Turf Moor, backed up with excellent away wins, 3-0 at West Ham United and 2-1 against the Baggies. The Clarets carried their winning form into April and completed a hat-trick of away wins as they secured a double over Watford with a 2-1 triumph at Vicarage Road.

The threat of Leicester City overtaking the Clarets was dealt with in the best possible way as goals from Wood and Kevin Long sealed a 2-1 victory over the Foxes at Turf Moor on April 14. The Clarets' outstanding five-game winning run was finally ended when Chelsea gained a level of revenge for their opening day defeat, with a 2-1 win at Turf Moor.

April ended with battling performances against relegation threatened Stoke and Brighton which provided two points and left the Clarets on the cusp of securing seventh place and European football. The point gained against the Seagulls resulted in Everton needing to win both of their final two games and make up a 15-goal deficit if they were going to overhaul Dyche's men.

The Toffees' draw at home to Southampton on Saturday 5 May ensured that Burnley would end the season in seventh place. And with two games to spare.

Although the campaign ended with defeats to Arsenal and Bournemouth, against all odds the Clarets had amassed 54 points and secured their best league finish in 43 years, while providing the fans with one of the club's most memorable seasons of the modern era.

KEVIN LONG MOBBED BY TEAMMATES AFTER SCORING THE SECOND V LEICESTER

CHRIS WOOD'S OPENER AGAINST THE FOXES

49

THE MOMENT

Defender Gary Parkinson struck the all-important Wembley winner that sealed the Clarets' promotion to the Endsleigh First Division in the 1994 Play-Off Final.

BURNLEY ARE BACK!

FIXTURE:	Second Division Play-Off Final
DATE:	Sunday 29 May 1994
SCORE:	Burnley 2-1 Stockport County
VENUE:	Wembley Stadium
ATTENDANCE:	44,806

Of the many promotion campaigns that Burnley Football Club have enjoyed over the years, their 1993/94 success will certainly live long in the memory for being the season they made it up ...but did it the hard way!

The regulation season ended with Jimmy Mullen's men scraping into the end-of-season Play-Off lottery with a sixth-place finish. The final league table saw the Clarets end the campaign an incredible twelve points shy of the two sides they would subsequently go on to defeat in the semi-final and then in the Wembley showpiece.

Plymouth Argyle provided the semi-final opposition and the first leg ended goalless at Turf Moor. The Clarets fell behind early in the second leg at Home Park, but produced a memorable comeback to win 3-1 and book a Wembley showdown with Stockport County.

Having suffered a defeat away to County and a draw at Turf Moor earlier in the season, it certainly proved to be a case of third time lucky for the Clarets - but once again with Burnley in 1993/94 it was never straightforward.

Just as in the semi-final, it was first blood to the opposition. The match could hardly have got off to a worse start from the Clarets' perspective as Stockport's Chris Beaumont guided a near-post header home after just two minutes play.

An ill-tempered affair saw County reduced to ten men after Michael Wallace was sent off having appeared to have spat at Ted McMinn.

Burnley levelled the match though David Eyres' sweetly struck curling effort after 29 minutes.

On the hour-mark Stockport scorer Beaumont was then sent off for a foul on Les Thompson and leaving the Hatters down to nine men.

On the vast Wembley pitch, Burnley soon made their numerical advantage count and after 66 minutes, Parkinson swept home a bobbling ball from the edge of the Stockport area. The goal sparked pandemonium among the large Burnley following who knew their heroes were going up!

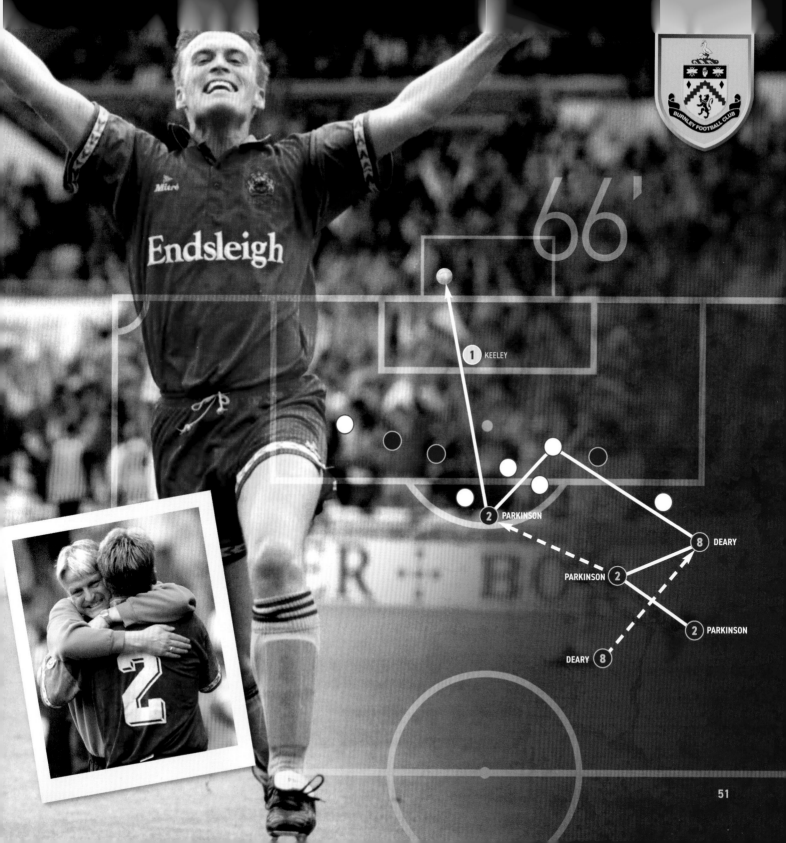

66'

1 KEELEY

2 PARKINSON

8 DEARY

PARKINSON 2

2 PARKINSON

DEARY 8

<<REWIND
QUIZ OF THE YEAR

The Clarets' 2017/18 campaign was certainly one to remember. So tackle these 20 teasers and see what you can recall...

6

Jack Cork was the club's top appearance maker in 2017/18. In all competitions, how many appearances did Jack make? Was it under 40, over 40 or 40 exactly?

1

Against which club did the Clarets record their first Premier League clean sheet of the season?

Chris Wood joined Burnley in August 2017 from Leeds Utd.

How many times had he netted in 2017/18 for the Whites before his transfer?

2

4

From which Premier League rival did Burnley secure the signing of Republic of Ireland international Jon Walters in the summer of 2017?

7 **Which opponent attracted the biggest crowd of the season to Turf Moor?**

9 Which defender returned to Turf Moor for a second stint with the Clarets in July 2017?

3

Who scored the club's first Premier League goal of the season?

5

Against which goalkeeper did Steven Defour net the Clarets' Goal of the Season?

8 Can you name the two Burnley players that were on target in the League Cup victory over local rivals Blackburn Rovers?

10

Who struck the only goal of the game to secure a Turf Moor victory over Newcastle Utd in October 2017?

52

11

Can you name the League One club that signed exciting young striker Dan Agyei on loan in August 2017?

13

At which ground did Nick Pope record his first away clean sheet in the Premier League?

12

After defeating Blackburn Rovers at Ewood Park in the second round of the League Cup, who were the Clarets paired with in the third round?

14

What was consistent about Burnley's matches both home and away against Premier League new boys Brighton and Huddersfield in 2017/18?

16

In which month did Sean Dyche win the manager of the month award?

15

Can you name the Burnley striker who scored in four consecutive Premier League games last season?

17

Against which club did Nahki Wells make his Clarets debut?

18

Who was the club's only permanent signing during the 2018 January transfer window?

19

Who scored the club's first goal of the calendar year of 2018?

20

Who netted the club's final goal of the season?

ANSWERS ON PAGE 82

53

The Clarets' faithful following have witnessed countless great goals over the years and while this selection may not be the definitive compilation of the club's best ten goals,

hopefully they will stir a few memories...

1. SAM VOKES

ABERDEEN 1-1 BURNLEY

UEFA EUROPA LEAGUE · 26 JULY 2019

Sam Vokes struck a vital equaliser as the Clarets made their long-awaited return to European football with a 1-1 draw at Aberdeen in the qualifying stages of the 2018/19 Europa League.

The meeting with the Dons provided an early season 'Battle of Britain' as Sean Dyche's men were paired with the Pittodrie club in the Second Qualifying Round of the competition.

Trailing to a soft first-half penalty, super-sub Vokes grabbed the all-important equaliser with 10 minutes remaining to tee things up perfectly for the second leg at Turf Moor.

So often the Clarets' goalscoring hero, the Wales international showed great strength and determination to bring Burnley level in the tie. James Tarkowski provided the delivery into the penalty area and when Chris Wood then picked out his strike partner, Vokes lifted the ball over his shoulder, shrugged off two defenders and volleyed an unstoppable effort past Joe Lewis and into the roof of the net.

It was another vital Vokes strike, with the popular Welshman making a habit of coming off the bench to inspire his team.

Vokes' historic goal - a first in Europe by a Burnley player since Brian Miller scored in both legs of the 1967 Fairs Cup defeat to Eintracht Frankfurt - sent the Clarets' travelling fans back home happy and ready to go again for the second leg a week later.

10 GREAT GOALS

2. STEPHEN WARD

CHELSEA 2-3 BURNLEY PREMIER LEAGUE · 12 AUGUST 2017

An absolute cracker from Stephen Ward doubled the Clarets' lead on the opening day of the 2017/18 season away to Premier League Champions Chelsea.

Sean Dyche's side produced a sparkling first-half performance at Stamford Bride in August 2017 to lead the match 3-0 at the interval. Sam Vokes netted twice but it was the superb strike from Ward that was sandwiched in between Vokes' brace that really caught the eye.

Ward's strike stunned the home crowd and things got even worse for the champions as Vokes added his second and Burnley's third just four minutes later.

The fixture computer had presented Burnley with the toughest of starts to the new campaign, and as expected Chelsea came back strongly after the break as goals from Alvaro Morata and David Luiz reduced deficit to a single goal.

However, the Clarets held out for the perfect start to the new season with a remarkable result and quality strike that really set the standard for the season ahead.

3. ANDRE GRAY

BURNLEY 4-0 BRISTOL CITY

CHAMPIONSHIP · 28 DECEMBER 2015

Andre Gray was the Clarets' hat-trick hero as Sean Dyche's side responded to a 3-0 Boxing Day defeat at promotion rivals Hull City with a 4-0 thrashing of Bristol City at Turf Moor.

The result was a perfect response to the defeat at the KC Stadium and ensured Burnley rounded off the calendar year of 2015 on a winning note. Gray grabbed the headlines for his hat-trick, but it was his first goal that opened the scoring which really was the pick of the bunch.

Keen to make instant amends for their previous performance, Burnley took the game to the visitors from the off and created a plethora of clear-cut chances in the opening 30 minutes. As opportunities came and went, the home crowd were beginning to get concerned that their heroes had not been able to convert their superiority into goals. Then, after 37 minutes, came a moment of magic from Gray. The all-action frontman gained possession inside the centre circle, turned and set off on a powerful surging run. After evading several defenders, he found himself just inside the penalty area and dispatched a beautiful curling effort past 'keeper Frank Fielding and into the bottom right-hand corner of the net.

With the deadlock broken, Gray helped himself to a second on the stroke of half-time and completed his treble with 12 minutes left on the clock. Scott Arfield was the other Burnley marksman in front of a crowd of 17,234.

4. ROBBIE BLAKE

BURNLEY 1-0 MANCHESTER UNITED

PREMIER LEAGUE · 19 AUGUST 2009

Not for the first time in his Burnley career, Robbie Blake was the toast of Tuft Moor. However, on this occasion his great goal sealed a historic Turf Moor victory over Premier League Champions Manchester United.

After winning promotion via the Play-Offs the previous season, all eyes were on the release of the 2009/10 fixtures as Burnley found themselves hosting the champions in their first home game of the season.

On what turned out to be an unforgettable night for the 20,872 packed into Turf Moor, it was Blake who scored the only goal of the game to seal a memorable Burnley victory with a fiercely struck shot. The match was just 19 minutes old when Blake lit up the contest with his thunderous effort. After a deep cross to the back post looking for Martin Patterson was headed partially clear by the United defence, Blake rushed in and hammered a shot right into the top corner of the net, leaving United 'keeper Ben Foster gasping at thin air.

Turf Moor erupted as Blake wheeled away in delight. The Clarets were forced to survive a few scares over the remainder of the evening before referee Alan Wiley signalled the end of what was a memorable occasion for the club and particularly for goalscorer Blake.

5. WADE ELLIOTT

BURNLEY 1-0 SHEFFIELD UNITED   CHAMPIONSHIP PLAY-OFF FINAL · 25 MAY 2009

"A bolt from the Claret and Blue" said the commentator as Wade Elliott struck the sweetest of strikes to open the scoring in the 2008/09 Championship Play-Off Final at Wembley.

Not only did Elliott's wonder-goal open the scoring, it also proved to be the only goal of a close-fought game that ultimately won the Clarets promotion to the Premier League.

The goal was just reward for Elliott who not only scored the goal but did so much to create the opportunity. The all-action midfielder was deep inside his own half when Martin Patterson played the ball to him after Patterson has done well to dispossess Kyle Naughton. Elliott then set off a surging run into the Blades' half and went through the gears as he skipped away from several challenges before playing in the

on-rushing Chris McCann. The Blades defence managed to block McCann's effort but the ball spun back to Elliott was positioned just outside the area and slightly to the left of the 'D' when he then proceeded to send a rocket-like shot past Paddy Kenny and into the top of the United goal.

Despite going into the match as slight underdogs, Owen Coyle's side showed great determination, organisation and skill to maintain their slender lead and bring top-flight football back to Turf Moor with a goal that was worthy of winning any game.

7. ANDY GRAY

BURNLEY 3-2 PRESTON NE
CHAMPIONSHIP · 27 OCTOBER 2006

A last-gasp goal from striker Andy Gray gave the Clarets all three points following a pulsating Lancashire derby match at Turf Moor in October 2006.

This topsy-turvy affair saw four goals scored in the final 13 minutes as Steve Cotterill's men came from behind to take the points thanks to Gray's late strike.

Visitors Preston has come into the fixture on the back on an impressive eleven-game unbeaten run, but it was Burnley who drew first blood when James O'Connor slotted them in front on the stroke of half-time.

Burnley were eventually pegged back when Simon Whaley equalised with a neat volley. Brett Ormerod then stunned Turf Moor and turned this derby clash on its head when he fired North End in front after shooting through a ruck of players with ten minutes remaining.

A strong finish to this Friday night thriller from the hosts led to Sean St Ledger heading into his own net under pressure from Gray following a teasing cross into the danger area. Gray then secured the headlines and the three points in the 89th minute with his seventh goal of the campaign.

Steve Jones sent in a cross from the left and Gray peeled away from his marker with a smart near-post run before directing a glancing header past Carlo Nash in the Preston goal.

6. ADE AKINBIYI

CHELSEA 1 BURNLEY 1
LEAGUE CUP · 12 NOVEMBER 2008

Ade Akinbiyi scored Burnley's second-half equaliser away to Chelsea in 2008 as the Clarets forced extra-time, before causing the upset of the round by knocking the big spending Londoners out of the League Cup after winning a penalty shoot-out 5-4.

Although the Clarets were enjoying an impressive Championship campaign, that would ultimately end in promotion glory, few outside of Turf Moor really fancied the team's chances when they were paired away to Chelsea despite having knocked Premier League Fulham out in the previous round.

When Didier Drogba showed his power to put the hosts a goal up after 27 minutes, a tough task got even harder. Against all odds, Burnley managed to keep themselves in the game and were rewarded for their efforts when Ade Akinbiyi scored a surprise equaliser midway through the second-half.

The goal came following neat approach play between Robbie Blake and Chris Eagles with the latter testing Carlo Cudicini with a stinging drive that the 'keeper did well to repel. However, Akinbiyi was on to the loose ball like a flash and slide it into an unguarded net to spark pandemonium among the 6,000 travelling Burnley supporters housed in the Shed End.

The score remained 1-1 after 90 minutes and after a further half an hour could not separate the two sides it came down to spot-kicks and a memorable 5-4 shoot out success for Burnley.

8. GLEN LITTLE

SCUNTHORPE 1-2 BURNLEY

DIVISION TWO · 6 MAY 2000

Burnley favourite Glen Little scored the winning goal at Glanford Park to spark mass celebrations as Stan Ternent's side secured promotion from the Second Division on the final day of the season.

This win saw Burnley gain automatic promotion in the most dramatic of circumstances as they reached second place in the table for the first time in the season and pipped Gillingham to the runners-up berth behind champions Preston.

Burnley travelled to Scunthorpe knowing they needed to better Gillingham's result if they were to take second place.

Despite going into the match already relegated, Scunthorpe took a 21st minute lead though Lee Hodges as they looked to cause a final day upset. Micky Mellon then levelled just before the break to set up an intriguing second half with all to play for, particularly with news filtering through that Gillingham were 1-0 down at Wrexham at half-time.

With 17 minutes left to play Burnley won a free-kick on the left side of the Scunthorpe area. The ball was clipped into the box by Paul Cook and cleared to the edge of the area where Little met the ball and cracked home a stunning winner. The goal sparked a mass pitch invasion from the a number of 2,500-strong travelling contingent who knew with Gillingham still trailing in North Wales their team were going up.

Little's goal was also met with delight at Turf Moor where 7,000 fans gathered on the Longside to watch the game on a giant screen.

60

9. IAN BRITTON

BURNLEY 2-1 ORIENT

DIVISION FOUR · 9 MAY 1987

Ian Britton etched his name into Burnley Football Club folklore by scoring arguably the most important goal of the Clarets' history.

On the final day of the 1986/87 season, Burnley faced the real threat of relegation from the Football League. The Clarets had suffered a difficult Fourth Division campaign and knew they had to defeat Play-Off chasing Orient at Turf Moor on the final day of the season to maintain their proud Football League status.

Ahead of what was to become one of the most memorable afternoon's that Turf Moor has ever witnessed, the atmosphere around the entire town was tense in the build-up to this do-or-die fixture.

The bumper crowd of 15,781 took a giant sigh of relief when Neil Grewcock put Burnley in front on the stroke of half-time.

However, three minutes into the second half and Turf Moor was rocked to its foundations as Ian Britton headed home Grewcock's cross to double the Clarets' lead. With the exception of the tiny pocket of Orient fans, the stadium went absolutely berserk as survival appeared in sight.

The nervy nature of the occasion increased when the visitors reduced the arrears through Alan Comfort to set up an almost unbearable ending for the on looking Burnley faithful. However, the Clarets held on and survived in the Football League at the expense of Lincoln City.

10. COLIN WALDRON

PRESTON NORTH END 1-1 BURNLEY

SECOND DIVISION · 28 APRIL 1973

In a match that is fondly remembered as one of the great Burnley games of the 1970s, defender Colin Waldron was the hero of the hour as his second-half equaliser at Deepdale secured the Second Division title for the Clarets.

The motives for success in this final day Lancashire derby could not have been more different. Burnley needed a point to pip QPR in the race for the Second Division title and win promotion back to the top flight after a two-year exile, while neighbours Preston needed the same to avoid relegation.

Inevitably, league leaders Burnley had the greater share of possession, but found Preston hard to break down. With Burnley stretched in their pursuit of an opening goal they were hit on the break as the ball fell for Alan Lamb, who ran 40 yards unopposed before shifting the ball on to strike partner Alex Bruce to fire past Alan Stevenson.

Paul Fletcher thought he had equalised early in the second half, but his header was cleared off the line. Other chances came and went, but with QPR ahead against Fulham, the Hoops had one hand on the Second Division trophy.

Ever-present defender Colin Waldron then picked the perfect moment to snatch the trophy back in Burnley's direction when he levelled with a 25-yard left-foot volley into the top corner.

61

U23 SQUAD

JOSH BENSON

POSITION: Midfielder **DOB:** 05/12/99

Cultured midfield playmaker Josh Benson joined the Clarets in the summer of 2018 following a two-year scholarship with Arsenal. Having initially joined the Gunners' Academy as an U9, Benson impressed in both training and U23 matches for Burnley in the later stages of 2017/18.

OLATUNDE BAYODE

POSITION: Winger **DOB:** 07/02/99

Attacking wideman Olatunde Bayode progressed through the Clarets' Academy to earn a two-year scholarship with the club. After impressing for the U18 team, he swiftly graduated to the U23 development squad and was rewarded with his first professional contract at the end of the 2017/18 season.

MARLEY BLAIR

POSITION: Midfielder **DOB:** 05/10/99

Following his release from the Liverpool Academy, winger Marley Blair impressed while on trial with Burnley and won an 18-month professional contract with the Clarets in January 2018. Born in Huddersfield, Blair chipped in with three goals for the U18 team last season and will be looking to impress at U23 level during the 2018/19 campaign.

ADAM BRUCE

POSITION: Goalkeeper **DOB:** 19/10/99

Promising young 'keeper Adam Bruce joined the Clarets back in 2011 after catching the eye in local football. A series of impressive displays for the U18 team in the 2017 Cee Cup in the Czech Republic landed him an award as the competition's top goalkeeper.

JAMES CLARKE

POSITION: Defender **DOB:** 02/04/00

Defender James Clarke has made rapid progress since joining Burnley as a 14-year-old. Involved with the U18 side while still a schoolboy, Clarke featured regularly for the U23 side in 2017/18. Last season was voted 'Scholar of the Year' and gained a call-up to the Republic of Ireland U19 squad.

TINASHE CHAKWANA

POSITION: Forward **DOB:** 25/10/98

Lively forward Tinashe Chakwana is another player to have progressed through the ranks at the Clarets' Academy. Top scorer for the U18s in 2016/17, he then repeated the trick for the U23 side last season. He signed his first professional contract at the end of 2017/18.

ED COOK

POSITION: Defender **DOB:** 22/11/99

Central defender Ed Cook put pen to paper on a professional contract at Turf Moor in July 2018 after completing his 'A' levels. After impressing during a trial period with Burnley, Cook returned to Berkshire to finish his studies before heading back to Burnley on a full-time basis.

U23 SQUAD

JORDAN CROPPER

POSITION: Defender   DOB: 12/05/00

Cropper joined the Clarets as a first-year scholar in February 2017. He linked up with Michael Duff's youth side towards the back end of the season, in their charge for the U18 Development League title. Despite joining the club as a forward, he currently plays right-back and in January 2018, he hit the winning goal at Turf Moor against Leeds United in the FA Youth Cup.

ANTHONY GLENNON

POSITION: Defender   DOB: 26/11/99

Left-sided defender Anthony Glennon joined the Clarets following a long spell with Liverpool Academy. Having played under Liverpool legend Steven Gerrard in the club's U18 side last season, Glennon is now relishing the opportunity of launching his senior career with the Clarets.

JIMMY DUNNE

POSITION: Defender   DOB: 19/10/97

Former Manchester United youngster Jimmy Dunne initially joined Burnley in July 2016. He gained useful first-team experience last season after joining Accrington Stanley on loan in January 2018. He enjoyed an outstanding run with the Reds and played his part in them landing the League Two title.

MACE GOODRIDGE

POSITION: Midfielder   DOB: 13/09/99

Mace Goodridge joined the Clarets in the summer of 2018 following an impressive spell with Michael Duff's U23 side at the tail end of the 2017/18 campaign. The midfielder had previously spent two seasons with Newcastle United and has also been in the youth ranks at Manchester City.

ROB HARKER

POSITION: Striker   **DOB:** 06/03/00

Young striker Rob Harker signed for the Clarets in July 2018 after leaving Bury. Harker had progressed through the youth ranks at Gigg Lane and made one first-team appearance for the Shakers. He trialled with the Clarets at the end of last season before securing a permanent deal.

ALI KOIKI

POSITION: Midfielder   **DOB:** 30/05/99

Defender Ali Koiki joined the Clarets in the summer of 2016 following a successful trial period with the club. He made the left-back berth his own at U23 level in 2017/18 and agreed his first professional contact at the end of last season.

MARK HOWARTH

POSITION: Defender   **DOB:** 22/08/99

Local boy Mark Howarth came through the Clarets' Academy and began his initial scholarship with the club in 2015. The Burnley-born midfielder was a regular face in both the U18 and U23 sides during the 2017/18 season.

NTUMBA MASSANKA

POSITION: Striker   **DOB:** 30/11/96

Born in Tottenham in November 1996, 6' 3" frontman Ntumba Massanka names both Manchester United and Manchester City among his former clubs. Since joining the Clarets in 2015, the striker has taken in valuable loan spells with York City, Morecambe and Wrexham.

65

U23 SQUAD

GEORGE McMAHON

POSITION: Goalkeeper   **DOB: 16/06/00**

The 18-year-old Republic of Ireland youth international penned a two-year professional contract - with the option of a further 12 months - at Turf Moor in August 2018. Manchester-born McMahon grew up in Hull and had a spell at Hull City after starting out in the youth set-up at York City. He then completed a two-year scholarship at Rotherham, making it as far as the bench for a third-round FA Cup tie in January, 2017.

CHRISTIAN N'GUESSAN

POSITION: Midfielder   **DOB: 20/10/98**

Having joined the Clarets from Blackpool in the summer of 2017, midfielder Christian N'Guessan was a regular in the U23 side during his first season at Tuff Moor. N'Guessan enjoyed success in the North West Youth Alliance and Lancashire FA Youth Cup while with Seasiders.

CONOR MITCHELL

POSITION: Goalkeeper   **DOB: 09/05/96**

Conor Mitchell progressed through the Clarets' Academy before turning professional in 2014. He has gained recognition with Northern Ireland at U19 and U12 level. After spending the first half of 2017/18 on loan with Chester City, he was a regular for the Clarets U23s once he returned to Turf Moor.

TEDDY PERKINS

POSITION: Defender   **DOB: 17/05/00**

Following his release from Leyton Orient, central defender Teddy Perkins impressed during a trial at Turf Moor at the end of last season and was handed a deal with the Clarets. A former captain of the Orient youth team, Perkins featured in a number of games for the Clarets at U23 level last season.

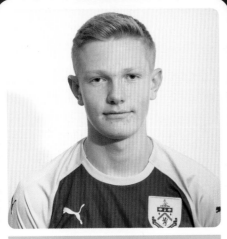

VINNIE STEELS

POSITION: Midfielder   **DOB:** 09/08/01

Steels linked up with the Clarets' U23 squad after agreeing a two-year deal with the club in the summer of 2018. He began his career at Sunderland before joining Darlington where he was a regular for the Quakers' reserve side. During the 2017/18 campaign, he enjoyed a spell with York City and made four first-team appearances for the Minstermen.

SCOTT WILSON

POSITION: Defender   **DOB:** 10/01/00

Powerful defender Scott Wilson joined the Clarets' youth set up back in 2013 after impressing for local junior sides. After gaining U23 experience in 2017/18, Wilson agreed an extension to his scholarship in the summer of 2018.

AIDEN STONE

POSITION: Goalkeeper   **DOB:** 20/07/99

A former England schools international, goalkeeper Aiden Stone was a regular member of the Clarets' U23 squad during the 2017/18 season, while also featuring for the U18 team. Stone agreed a new twelve-month deal at Turf Moor at the end of last season.

OLLIE YOUNGER

POSITION: Defender   **DOB:** 14/11/99

Burnley supporter Ollie Younger was voted the Youth Team Player of the Year at the end of his first season as a scholar in 2016/17. He became a regular for the U23 side last season and agreed his first professional contract in the summer of 2018.

67

JIMMY ADAMSON

PAUL FLETCHER

SPOT THE SEASON

Burnley ended this season as Second Division champions and brought to an end their brief two-season spell away from Division One.

Under the management of Jimmy Adamson and his assistant Brian Miller, the Clarets held off the challenge of Queens Park Rangers to return to the top-flight as Second Division champions. Adamson built this title-winning side on the foundations of the club's 1967/68 FA Youth Cup-winning team and made some shrewd signings to strengthen the squad along the way.

Paul Fletcher was the team's leading scorer with 15 goals, as a determined and resolute group of players lost just four games all season - two at home and two away. They clinched the title with a Colin Waldron goal securing a point away in a 1-1 draw at Preston North End on the final day of the season.

Can you name the season?

Thumped 4-1 away to Sheffield Wednesday on the opening day of the season, Burnley then ended this campaign with a Wembley victory over Wednesday's city rivals United in the Championship Play-Off Final to secure promotion to the Premier League.

Under the guidance of Owen Coyle, the Clarets enjoyed a memorable campaign with a fifth-place finish and a shot at Play-Off glory.

Martin Paterson was the club's top scorer and he was on target in the Play-Off semi-finals as Burnley secured a 3-0 aggregate success over Reading and a Wembley date with the Blades.

A memorable goal from Wade Elliott won the day for the Clarets at Wembley and sparked mass celebrations for the thousands decked in Claret and Blue as Burnley headed back to the big time.

Can you name the season?

2

3

Under the management of Harry Potts, Burnley secured a 12th-place finish in the First Division as one of four clubs who all ended the season with 42 points.

Northern Ireland international Willie Irvine ended the campaign as the club's leading scorer with 25 goals.

The Clarets enjoyed an exciting FA Cup run which saw them dispatch Brentford and Reading before facing Manchester United at Old Trafford in the fifth Round.

Andy Lochhead gave the Clarets a 17th minute and the visitors held their advantage until the 81st minute when Denis Law levelled for United. With a Turf Moor replay on the looking on the card, Pat Crerand then grabbed a winner for United to break Burnley hearts.

Despite the late heartbreak at Old Trafford, Potts' men bounced back in the best possible way - winning 4-1 away to Blackburn Rovers in the First Division just four days later.

Can you name the season?

ANSWERS ON PAGE 82.

ICON

IN CLARET AND BLUE

A real case of 'local boy made good' - a boyhood Burnley fan, Micky Phelan went on to play with distinction for the Clarets and starred in the club's 1981/82 Third Division title-winning season.

Born in Nelson in 1962, Phelan joined Burnley as an associate schoolboy before progressing though the youth and reserve ranks at Turf Moor. He turned professional with his beloved Burnley in June 1980.

Phelan's Clarets debut arrived during his first season as a pro when he entered the fray as a substitute in Burnley's 3-0 Third Division defeat away to Chesterfield on Saturday 31 January 1982. A Turf Moor bow came a week later when he started the Clarets' 1-0 victory over Exeter City.

That home debut against the Grecians saw Phelan operate in the centre of defence, a role he played for the majority of his Burnley career. However, he did show his versatility by also operating in central midfield when needed - a position he really excelled in later in his career at Norwich City and Manchester United.

The 1981/82 season saw Phelan as a recognised first-team starter in what was a young defensive unit marshalled by experienced goalkeeper Alan Stevenson. The campaign was a memorable one as Burnley lifted the Third Division title and won promotion to the Second Division.

Despite the Clarets suffering relegation in 1982/83 and an immediate return to the Third Division, the team enjoyed impressive runs in both cup competitions. A memorable League Cup campaign saw them reach the semi-final stage before bowing out to eventual winners Liverpool. In a season that provided memorable cup clashes and a spirited, but ultimately unsuccessful, battle for Second Division survival - Phelan was ever-present in both league and cup. His consistent performances saw him land the Supporters' Club Player of the Year and Young Player of the Year awards come the end of the 1982/83 season.

Phelan proved to be the club's star player over the next two seasons, but after the Clarets suffered relegation to the Fourth Division in 1985, it became clear that his time was up at Turf Moor. His talents deserved better than Fourth Division football and such were the club's finances at the time that they needed to cash in on one of their more saleable assets.

In July 1985, Phelan joined Norwich City for a fee of £70,000. In his first season at Carrow Road he helped the Canaries secure an immediate return to the top-flight as they won the Second Division title at a canter.

Phelan soon established himself as one of the First Division's top midfielder's while at Carrow Road and captained the Canaries to the 1988-89 FA Cup semi-final and a fourth placed league finish.

In the summer of 1989, Phelan secured a dream move to Manchester United. His £750,000 switch to Old Trafford triggered a trophy-laden spell for Phelan and the beginning of the most successful era in United's rich history. During his time playing for United, Phelan won the FA Cup, European Cup Winners' Cup, League Cup and a Premier League title.

His playing days ended at West Bromwich Albion before he embarked on a highly successful and well documented career in coaching and management. However, of the four clubs he played for - he made more league appearances for Burnley than any of the others.

FULL NAME:	Michael Christopher Phelan
DATE OF BIRTH:	24 September 1962
PLACE OF BIRTH:	Nelson
POSITION:	Midfielder

BURNLEY APPEARANCES		BURNLEY GOALS	
211		**13**	
LEAGUE:	168	LEAGUE:	9
FA CUP:	16	FA CUP:	0
LEAGUE CUP:	16	LEAGUE CUP:	2
OTHER:	11	OTHER:	2

DEBUT: **Chesterfield 3 Burnley 0**
31 January 1981 · Division Three

ENGLAND

APPEARANCES	GOALS
1	**0**

DEBUT: **England 0 Italy 0**
15 November 1989

MIKE
PHELAN

SECOND YEARS

KAI CALDERBANK-PARK

POSITION: Goalkeeper

Stopper Kai Calderbank-Park made the move from Australia to England to pursue his career in football. He began his scholarship in the summer of 2017 and having now recovered from a long-term back problem he will be looking to star for the U18 team in 2018/19.

WILL HARRIS

POSITION: Striker

Hailing from the North-East, Will Harris has been converted from defender to striker and joined Burnley as a scholar in July 2017. In September 2018 he joined Nelson on a work experience loan deal.

DYLON ALLAN-MEREDITH

POSITION: Midfielder

Winger Dylon Allan-Meredith began his two-year scholarship with the Clarets in 2017. A tricky winger, he played on a regular basis for the U16 side before joining the club on a full-time basis.

MICHAEL FOWLER

POSITION: Striker

Striker Michael Fowler ended last season as the top scorer for the U18 side with nine goals in his first season as a full-time scholar. In September 2018 he joined Padiham on a work experience loan and has been in goalscoring for the Storks in the early part of 2018/19.

ETHAN KERSHAW

POSITION: Midfielder

Central midfielder Ethan Kershaw was ever-present for the U18s last season during the first year of his scholarship. The teenager was appointed the U18's vice-captain at the start of the 2018/19 campaign.

DAN MOSS

POSITION: Defender

Defender Dan Moss progressed through several ranks of the Clarets' Academy set-up before agreeing a two-year scholarship in July 2017. A versatile performer, Moss can operate anywhere across the back four and also in a midfield role.

RICHARD TAYLOR

POSITION: Defender

Giant defender Richard Taylor began his two-year scholarship with Burnley in the summer of 2017. After featuring in the under-18 side on an occasional basis last season, he joined Colne on loan in September 2018.

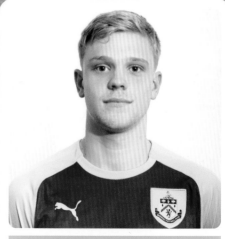

OSCAR WOODS

POSITION: Midfielder

Talented Australian midfielder Oscar Woods joined the Clarets in July 2017 but has had to wait for international clearance from the FA before he can feature in competitive fixtures. Woods has performed well in both training and friendly matches.

TERRY MUPARIWA

POSITION: Midfielder

A regular face in the U18 team during his first year as a scholar in 2017/18, midfielder Terry Mupariwa netted his first goal for Burnley against Leeds United in January 2018.

BOBBY THOMAS

POSITION: Defender

Previously with the Everton Academy, defender Bobby Thomas joined the Clarets in the summer of 2017 following his release from the Toffees. The defender also has an eye for goal, scoring three times for the under-18s last season.

KIAN YARI

POSITION: Midfielder

Midfielder Kain Yari was on the books of both Manchester City and Manchester United before spending six year progressing through the Clarets' Academy. The skilful playmaker began his two-year scholarship in July 2017.

U18 FIRST-YEARS SQUAD

JOE CONLEY
POSITION: Midfielder

Talented central midfielder Joe Conley joined the Clarets' Academy set-up in July 2018. Having previously been on the books at Everton, Conley is a former teammate of second-year scholar Bobby Thomas.

HARRY ALLEN
POSITION: Goalkeeper

Goalkeeper Harry Allen joined the Clarets' Academy ahead of the 2018/19 campaign after leaving Manchester United. The 6' 2" shot-stopper featured on the bench for the U18 side on a number of occasions last season.

UDOKA CHIMA
POSITION: Defender

Following a successful trial with the Clarets, Udoka Chima joined the Burnley Academy in the summer of 2018. This 16-year-old defender was spotted playing grassroots football in North London and trialled with a number of league clubs before settling on a career path at Burnley.

RHYS FENLON
POSITION: Striker

Striker Rhys Fenlon played regularly for the U16 side in 2017/18 and accepted the Clarets' offer of a two-year scholarship in the summer of 2018. Not a player to get on the wrong side of - Fenlon also holds six Thai-Boxing titles including three British Champion belts!

74

MITCHELL GEORGE

POSITION: Forward

After displaying a great eye for goal while playing local football, Mitchell George netted three times in six games for the Clarets' U16 side last season. He joined the Burnley Academy in July 2018 ahead of the 2018/19 campaign.

MATTHEW O'NEILL

POSITION: Forward

Liverpool-born wide-man Matthew O'Neill has come through the Clarets' Academy and agreed a two-year scholarship in July 2018. He was a regular member for the U16 side in 2017/18 and also stepped up to the U18s as the season progressed.

EDON PRUTI

POSITION: Defender

Towering central defender has linked up with the Clarets following his release from Stevenage. He agreed his two-year scholarship with Burnley back in May 2018 and got life with the Clarets underway in July.

JAYDON MAJOR

POSITION: Forward

Winger Jaydon Major joined Burnley midway through the 2017/18 campaign and made a number of substitute appearances for the youth team last season. He began his two-year scholarship in the summer of 2018.

KANE PATTERSON

POSITION: Defender

Right-back Kane Patterson earned an international call-up to the Scotland U16 squad last season and having been on the books at Tottenham Hotspur, he joined the Clarets in 2018. Kane's older brother, Phoenix, is a second-year scholar at Tottenham Hotspur.

MATTY RAIN

POSITION: Defender

Left-back Matty Rain was another player to spend 2017/18 with the Clarets and step up to feature in last season's youth team. He began his scholarship in July 2018 after being offered terms at the end of the previous season.

FAST FORWARD >>

Do your predictions for 2018/19 match our own?...

PREMIER LEAGUE WINNERS

Liverpool

PREMIER LEAGUE TOP SCORER

Harry Kane

PREMIER LEAGUE RUNNERS-UP

Manchester City

RELEGATED TO THE CHAMPIONSHIP IN 18TH

Southampton

RELEGATED TO THE CHAMPIONSHIP IN 19TH

Fulham

BOTTOM OF THE PREMIER LEAGUE

Newcastle United

FA CUP WINNERS

Burnley

FA CUP RUNNERS-UP

Manchester United

LEAGUE CUP WINNERS

Arsenal

LEAGUE CUP RUNNERS-UP

Chelsea

BURNLEY FOOTBALL

CHAMPIONSHIP WINNERS

Leeds United

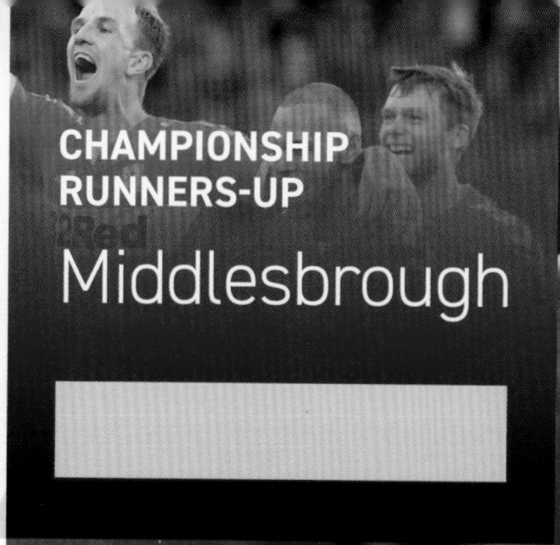

CHAMPIONSHIP RUNNERS-UP

Middlesbrough

CHAMPIONSHIP PLAY-OFF WINNERS

Derby County

CHAMPIONSHIP TOP SCORER

Neal Maupay

Brentford

THE CLARETS' TOP SCORER

Sam Vokes

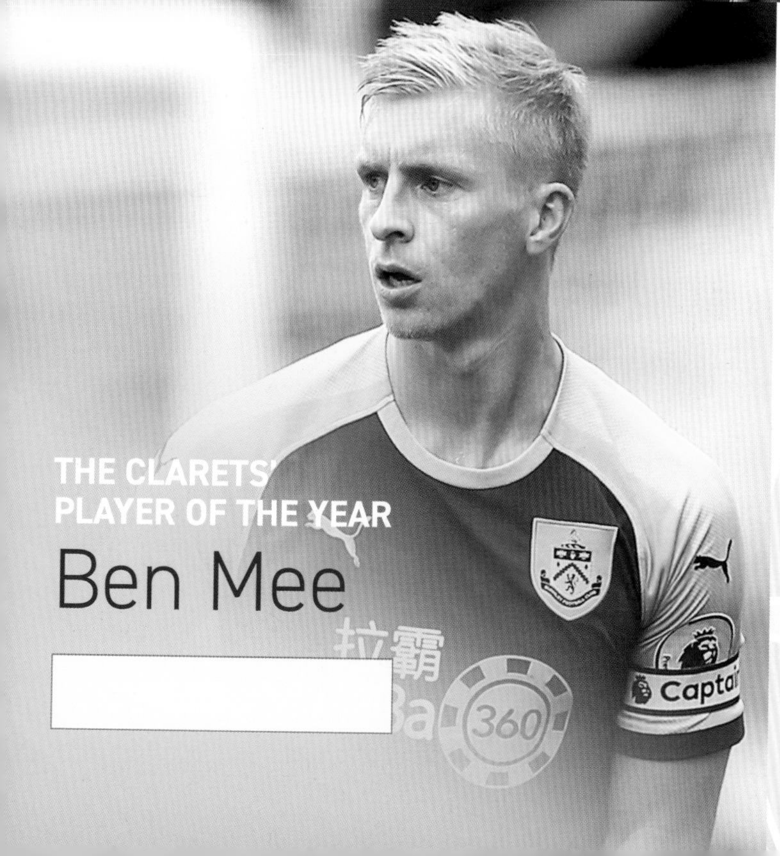

THE CLARETS' PLAYER OF THE YEAR

Ben Mee

CHAMPIONS LEAGUE WINNERS

Juventus

CHAMPIONS LEAGUE RUNNERS-UP

Barcelona

EUROPA LEAGUE WINNERS

Arsenal

EUROPA LEAGUE RUNNERS-UP

AC Milan

77

BURNLEY FC WOMEN

3-0 WINNERS OVER MORECAMBE LFC

BACK (L TO R): 15 Jade Foster DF, 11 Linny Craig MF, 17 Natalie Bell MF, 6 Samantha Fleck DF, 1 Lauren Bracewell GK, 9 Justine Wallace MF, 16 Katie Halligan MF, 2 Dani Cooper DF, 13 Evie Priestley FW.

Burnley FC Women was established in 1995, now operated by Burnley FC in the Community, Burnley FC Women provides elite training and development to players from U6 to Senior Women's teams.

Burnley FC Women has seen significant change over the last year. In May 2018, the club was officially rebranded with a new name, logo and website designed to highlight Burnley FC in the Community's commitment and vision for female football at the club.

At the end of the 2017/18 season, the Burnley FC Women first team were promoted to the FA Women's National League Northern Division 1. The title win, the first in eleven years, will see the side compete in the Women's FA National League, for the first time.

The First Team's league season kicked off in August with a loss against Chester-le-street Town Ladies and a draw against Leeds United Ladies as the team adapted to the higher division. However, in September, they went on a great run, winning six consecutive games in all competitions and scoring 13 goals along the way with only four goals conceded.

The team took maximum points in the league fixtures against established teams, Liverpool Feds Women, Bolton Wanderers Ladies, Norton & Stockton Ancients LFC and Barnsley FC Ladies. As a result, Burnley sat proudly at the top of the table, an achievement that many would not have deemed possible at the start of the season for a newly promoted side.

The winning league run continued with an early October 3-0 victory against Morecambe Ladies FC. The future looks bright for Burnley FC Women.

BURNLEY FC WOMEN

HAMER & EMBLEY CELEBRATE V LIVERPOOL FEDS LFC

FRONT (L TO R): 12 Nicola Shirtcliffe DF, 10 Sarah Greenhalgh FW, 8 Elizabeth Hamer MF, 5 Jo Holt (Captain) DF, 3 Vikki Eastwood DF, 7 Leah Embley FW. NOT PICTURED: 4 Charlotte Banner MF.

DANNY DELIVERS!

FIXTURE:	Sky Bet Championship
DATE:	Sunday 9 March 2014
SCORE:	Blackburn Rovers 1 Burnley 2
VENUE:	Ewood Park
ATTENDANCE:	21,589

During the Clarets' 2013/14 promotion-winning season, it was the long-awaited victory over arch-rivals Blackburn Rovers that provided the standout moment of a classic campaign.

Sunday 9 March 2014 will always be remembered fondly for all connected with the Clarets, as after a 35-year spell, Burnley finally ended their wait for a derby day triumph.

Sean Dyche's men were in pursuit of league leaders Leicester City and in need of victory to keep their promotion push intact. While bitter-rivals Rovers were pushing for a top-six finish and a Play-Off place. Suffice to say, the stakes could not have been much higher for this eagerly-awaited local derby.

Rovers took the lead through Jordan Rhodes after 24 minutes, but Burnley produced a stirring second-half comeback to the delight of the travelling fans among a crowd of 21,589 at Ewood Park.

A rare goal from defender Jason Shackell drew the Clarets level after 73 minutes and six minutes later Danny Ings completed the turnaround to put Burnley in front.

In a frantic ending to the match, Rovers pushed hard for an equaliser and the final minutes certainly felt like hours for the watching Burnley faithful. Despite some real 'heart-in-mouth' moments during four minutes of injury-time, Burnley held on for an historic win. The scenes at the final whistle will live long in the memory for all of a Claret and Blue persuasion.

Victory over Blackburn was sweet and the icing on the cake soon followed as the team and went on to seal automatic promotion behind the Foxes. Rovers meanwhile fell short of a place in the end-of-season Play-Offs.

THE MOMENT

Danny Ings finally ended the Clarets' 35-year-long wait for a derby-day victory over arch-rivals Blackburn Rovers

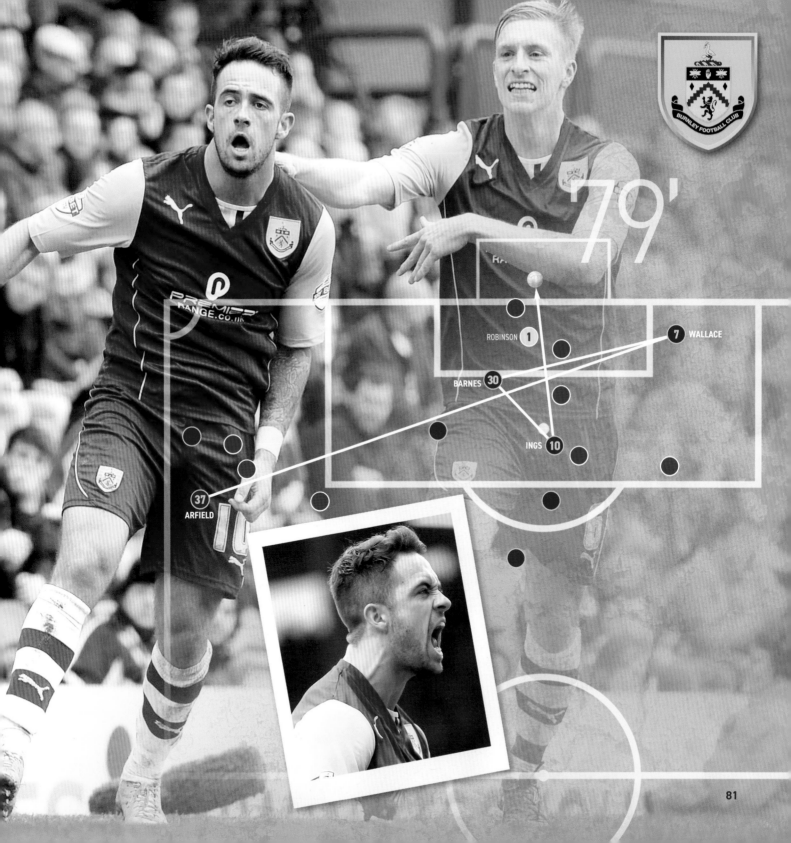

'79'

ROBINSON **1**

7 WALLACE

BARNES **30**

INGS **10**

37
ARFIELD

ANSWERS

PAGE 52:
<<REWIND QUIZ OF THE YEAR

1. Crystal Palace.
2. Once.
3. Sam Vokes.
4. Stoke City.
5. David de Gea.
6. Over 40 (41 in total).
7. Manchester United.
8. Jack Cork & Robbie Brady.
9. Phil Bardsley.
10. Jeff Hendrick.
11. Walsall.
12. Leeds United.
13. Goodison Park (Everton).
14. All four games failed to produce a goal.
15. Ashley Barnes.
16. March.
17. Tottenham Hotspur.
18. Aaron Lennon.
19. Johann Berg Gudmundsson (v Liverpool).
20. Chris Wood.

PAGE 68:
SPOT THE SEASON

1. 1972/73.
2. 2008/09.
3. 1964/65.